To
Nancy,
You are never alone
when reading a book.

Love
Arthur
Molinari

# THE LITTLE BOY WHO LISTENED

**By the same author**

*The Little Dutch Boy*, The Book Guild, 1993

# THE LITTLE BOY WHO LISTENED

*Portrait of a Medium*

Ronald Hearn

Book Guild Publishing
Sussex, England

First published in Great Britain in 2008 by
The Book Guild Ltd
Pavilion View
19 New Road
Brighton BN1 1UF

Second Printing 2008

Typesetting in Times by
Keyboard Services, Luton, Bedfordshire

Printed in Great Britain by
CPI Antony Rowe

A catalogue record for this book is available from
The British Library

ISBN 978 1 84624 212 0

# *Contents*

# *Acknowledgements for contributions and help*

Peter Ingold

Lady Baden Powell

Cheryl Barrymore

Dorit Chomer

John Copley

Wendy Crane

Jean Craven

Zainab Dayekh

Sir Clifford Fisher

Tara Newley

Fay Ostrom

Peta Pryor

and to Robert Anderson for his excellent help in editing the manuscript

# 1

## *Prologue*

Arthur Molinary is a larger than life character, a jolly man who tells a stream of jokes and amusing tales, and is not what one would imagine a medium to be.

*Gibraltar Chronicle*, 28 September, 2004

This is a perfect description of a man who, in my opinion, is one of the finest psychics I know. Being hailed as 'Gibraltar's own medium' pleases Arthur Molinary greatly, as he still has a very strong attachment to the place of his birth. He can now be hailed as one of England's own, having lived in that country with his family for a number of years, although he visits Gibraltar whenever he can. This is the story of a little boy who, as he grew to manhood, listened and learnt a lot, in order to become an extraordinary medium. It also, I hope, gives an insight into the mind of a medium and into how communication with another world can take place.

My first impression of Arthur on seeing him at the London Spiritual Mission was of a very quiet and shy young man, very good looking with big eyes and an even bigger smile. He did not initially strike me as anyone outstanding but I soon changed my mind. My own purpose in being there that evening was to give an address and demonstration of clairvoyance, or so it was billed. In fact, it was a talk on the subject followed by a demonstration of communication between two worlds, earthly and spiritual, in order to give evidence of survival and the continuation of life. Arthur had been involved with the subject all of his life, but had not done much with the inborn gift he obviously had. He had been a member of the London Spiritual Mission for a considerable time and, whilst helping out in the church, had listened to many other mediums. Sometimes he acted as chairman for the services held there, and later became Vice-President for a time. Most Spiritualist churches follow a similar pattern to many non-conformist Christian churches, the main difference being inclusion of a demonstration of clairvoyance.

I learnt he had a system of awarding marks to each medium who worked there. At first he gave me 'eight out of ten' for my performance, but later I hit the target and scored a bullseye, 'ten out of ten'. This showed me that, right from the start, he was a perfectionist, which I warmed to, being one myself. Being a perfectionist does not mean one is always right, but that one is striving to be totally accurate in transmitting evidence from the other world. Arthur always displayed a dogged determination to get it right, along with complete honesty. With him, what he sees and hears is exactly what you get. Which became obvious later when I witnessed his chairmanship. He has a wonderful way of winning people over.

On subsequent visits to the Mission I found him becoming more friendly; he was as always, very polite. It felt to me, however, as though he was hiding his light under a bushel. One could not help but like this young man, Gibraltarian by birth, with a mother who was a Spanish Moor and a Jewish Genoese father. He had inherited so much from his mixed blood, including a great sense of humour, along with a creative and artistic ability. He joked that his heritage had given him mixed blessings. It was not long before I realised this man had a great gift which needed to be brought out and used.

Each time I visited the Mission along with my friend Peter Ingold, the friendship between the three of us grew. This resulted in Arthur coming to Peter's home where many interesting discussions took place. At that time Arthur worked as a book restorer in a very small firm in Kilburn. He did some very fine bookbinding that enabled him to utilise his creative and artistic talent. Mostly he worked alone and had become very depressed by it, feeling the job would go nowhere. Even so, his work was of beautiful quality. Fortunately, his psychic ability was beginning to emerge and would eventually take him off on a new track. I had experienced the same thing some years earlier, as after many frustrating years in the same job, my psychic gifts became too strong, leaving me no choice but to leave and embark on a full-time mission to help others.

For Arthur, it transpired that he gave up his job in order to look after his sick mother. It was after her passing to the other world that he felt the desire to use his gift in order to help others. Deep down inside he is a very caring man and for him the call had come not a moment too soon. I believe that our lives are pre-planned and usually everything happens at the right time and in the right way for each individual. Arthur asked me to help him in any way I could. Having already realised his great potential and the possibility of a great future ahead if he was prepared to go for it, I accepted the challenge on condition he would do as I taught him until he was able to do things his way. The art of teaching is to pass on one's experience and knowledge to others; when they pass out they are entitled to do as they will with it.

First, I explained how I worked and my experience as to how the psychic functions, at the same time telling him he would inevitably develop his own style and approach. I had no need to advise him about honesty: with Arthur there are few frills and superficial embellishments, just a lot of plain speaking. Too many mediums abuse the gifts they have; they are not always honest and sometimes even devious. It was a relief to me that Arthur felt as I did and still do and would work in much the same way. In my work I have always felt I do not wish to mislead anyone, least of all myself. A medium's work is to try to give evidence of survival and an assurance of an afterlife, as well as comfort and advice to those in need. It is a huge responsibility. It is possible for some psychics to concentrate purely on predictions or fortune-telling. Arthur will have none of this.

With the help of Peter I decided to do some experiments which possibly would be rather difficult for Arthur. If successful, it would show just how psychic Arthur was. I have done a lot of experiments and worked in an unusual way because I feel challenge is necessary to bring out the best in us. Peter and I had friends and relatives who, having passed on, could now provide good evidence if successful contact was made. We decided on some names and wrote them down on slips of paper, which we then put into plain envelopes. I asked Arthur to hold them one at a time and give whatever impressions and feelings he received. We did not really expect too much but Arthur came up with some amazing results. There was absolutely nothing other than a name inside each envelope so he could not see anything to give him any clues whatsoever.

The most impressive results came when he held an envelope containing the name Margaret Burton. He immediately saw in his mind a beautiful blonde lady with very large eyes who was vivacious and full of life. He heard her singing and felt she must have been on the stage. He then relayed many details and incidents which left us in no doubt it was Margaret communicating. The finest evidence came when he said she was insisting he tell us she was wearing a big black cloak, the emphasis being on the word 'big'.

4

The last time we saw Margaret was in London's St Martin's Lane where she was starring in a revival of the musical *Oliver*. We had spotted a lady wearing a voluminous black cloak and waving to us from across the road. We crossed over and were delighted to find under that cloak was our dear friend Margaret, whom we had not seen for some time. As bubbly and delightful as ever, she explained she was wearing her theatrical costume as she was on a break and needed to pop out for some fresh air. She was exactly as Arthur described: blonde and bubbly, one of the loveliest ladies we've known. The only difference since we last saw her was that she had gained a lot of weight, hence the accent on 'big'. She was a glorious singer equally at home in grand opera at the Coliseum as she was in *Oliver*. One could never forget her big sparkling eyes and her being so 'full of life'. It was a shock to learn of her early passing but good to know she was alive and well in the other world.

Peter wrote his paternal grandmother's name on a slip and, as far as Arthur was concerned, he could see nothing but a blank envelope. At that time, despite being friends, Arthur knew very little of either of our backgrounds and certainly would not have known anything about Peter's grandparents and relatives who had long since passed. Almost immediately he described a very thin woman with a long and rather lined face. She had shoulder-length brown curly hair and was very self-willed. Peter told Arthur this did not fit the description of the person named. Arthur asked if he could try again to get clarification and then said Peter should know her and she was called May. Peter immediately realised it was an excellent description of his grandmother's sister, Mabel, whom everyone called May. Once recognised, May and his grandmother gave a wealth of evidence to Peter showing they had survived and were still taking an interest in family and friends left behind.

Another name given to Arthur was 'May Wood', a friend

who had lived in Bognor Regis in Sussex. I laughed when Arthur told me she lived just up the road from the station and rode a full-sized tricycle. She was a well-known figure riding around Bognor. She then mentioned her love of watching snooker on television and passion for fast cars, and gave details of her tiny house where she had some Delft china on the wall and a Union Jack over the front door. This was quite extraordinary evidence as she had often said she would 'put the flags out' when I went to visit her. I had known May through my work but had not met her personally until I finally made the journey with Peter. When we located her house, just up from the station, we did indeed find the front door covered by a huge Union Jack. On this visit we also saw the Delft china on the wall. May never stopped talking: about the snooker she so loved and her interest in racing cars; she had even once driven one herself.

There were other names sealed in envelopes from which Arthur was able to give much evidence, but these particular examples showed his mediumship was already outstanding both in quality and quantity. Although Peter and I were good friends of Arthur, neither of us was prepared to say yes to anything unless it was true. Some people when consulting mediums are inclined to say no to everything in order to make the medium work harder and give more. It serves no purpose except to make a mockery of the subject.

After these experiments I could only agree it was time for Arthur to be 'launched', so to speak. Having myself worked for a time at the College of Psychic Studies I could only feel that it would be the best place for him to flourish. I telephoned the secretary and explained about this young man with an exceptional gift whom I could highly recommend and who was eager to work. As I was known and respected there, they were more than happy to give him an audition.

On the due date I went along with him and after introductions were completed the secretary took him to another room so he could give her a sitting, or 'reading' as Arthur prefers to call it. When they returned an hour later I knew all was well. She explained that, although she had no doubts that Arthur would be accepted to work at the College, she would first have to report to the committee. A few days later he received his invitation to work there and he has now been at the College for many years. He is highly sought after by people of all kinds, including celebrities from various fields as well as the general public. He has also developed various ways of expressing his gifts, about more of which we will hear later.

The above tells how Arthur Molinary was discovered and began his work. Equally fascinating is the story of his life so far as told to me by him.

# 2

## *Early Days*

Arthur's background made up from many different ingredients and the Mediterranean cultures that fashioned his ancestry and character have made him a very interesting and somewhat unusual man. Although he has been labelled as a 'medium', 'psychic' and 'clairvoyant' he does not think of himself as any of these but simply as a listener who pays attention to his own thoughts and feelings. He listens to what others think and say and has done so since childhood. This may seem strange, as all the above labels actually do apply to him, but he refuses to be pigeonholed. Knowing him as I do, I sympathise with his point of view. Psychic abilities of any kind should only be expressed as honestly as one can, not according to artificial categories imposed from the outside.

Arthur Molinary was born in Gibraltar on the 12th January 1945. Psychic ability was there in his blood.

Arthur's mother, Cecilia, was very psychic and she was beaten black and blue by her father because of it. Being someone who would never keep her mouth shut she suffered a lot more but never let go of her belief in the psychic. When she was eleven years old, and working as a shepherdess, she started seeing visions. When she used to go on her walks she would go past an old Moorish ruin, where an old man would beckon her and show her a place where she was to dig. She told her mother and sisters but when her father got to hear about it, he became angry. Talk of spirits and an unknown world made him hostile. Some time later Arthur's grandmother's brother, Silvestre, who believed in communication between the two worlds, went and dug where Arthur's mother had indicated. He found large marble slabs, gold coins and other objects. He became rich overnight. Some other family members were interested and active in the subject and Arthur later learnt a great deal from them. There is an old saying, 'the looker-on sees most of the game', and we might add that 'the listener hears more'.

A few years before his birth his mother, Cecilia, and sister, Jeronima, had been evacuated from their home owing to the Second World War when Gibraltar became a full-time military base. They were shipped out to London and housed in the Grand Hotel in Putney where they suffered three years of war before being moved to another hotel in Oxford Street. They returned home in 1944 when they were reunited with Arturo, Cecilia's husband. It was soon after this that Arthur was conceived and born. Despite his mixture of Spanish and Italian blood he was nonetheless a Gibraltarian and consequently a British subject.

Arthur was a delicate child, sensitive intuitive and aware – important factors, no doubt, in his psychic development. He began his life with an allergy to milk and the lymph glands in his neck were operated on and removed. He refused to swallow any kind of milk, but his family got around that problem by adding sugar to it. When he was old enough he was made to drink goat's milk. This was obtained from a goatman who came round the houses with his three goats selling the still-warm milk. His grandmother would buy a daily jug for him to drink.

His own memories of Gibraltar start in his parent's second home, which was at 9 Horse Barracks Lane, and where sometime between the ages of three and four he experienced his first illness. He caught measles and developed various complications including temporary paralysis. He had to be kept in a darkened bedroom as his eyes had grown too sensitive to light. Despite many problems in early life, such as lack of money to pay for medicines, he was well looked after by his parents. Others in the family also helped. On one occasion his godmother went to the Sisters of Charity, who sent a nun to administer a much-needed daily injection that his parents could not otherwise afford. Arthur does not remember the nun's name but has never forgotten her sweet face and encouraging words. He made up his mind that if he got well again he would become a priest and do what she did for others. Luckily for the world in general he did not. Instead he became the caring and helpful man that he is: as a medium, he helps anyone and everyone of any faith, and with the spiritual freedom to express himself as he feels and senses.

At one time the young Arthur had to lay in a darkened room because of an illness. All he could do was listen to noises coming from outside, such as his mother working around the house or talking to neighbours, or his mother's favourite flamenco music playing on the radio. One of the sounds he loved most of all was that of his mother pouring water into a large jar called a *tinaja*, an earthenware container used for storing water. As the house had no water supply, it had to be filled with water from an outside pump.

He found great strength from the occasions the nun visited him. They talked about God and whether there was such a person or thing. One time she gave him a picture of a little boy and girl playing near the edge of a cliff, watched over by a guardian angel with outstretched wings. He still has this picture stuck in his Bible as a reminder of the divine force that helped the nun help him. This was to be the basis of his great belief and strength in the power of love and healing that can be given and received. The kind nun's words of comfort would become the basis for his life's work.

After this illness he spent a lot of time between the ages

of four and nine going between his parents' home and that of his grandmother in La Linea, just across the border in Spain. She lived in a street called La Vista Alegre, which means 'the happy view'. On one visit she took him to a photographer to have his portrait taken for a visa that would allow him to stay in La Linea as long as he needed.

Grandmother's house was a bedsit and kitchen within a small patio complex with five other neighbours. The house was simply furnished and fairly sparse. Cooking was done on charcoal and now, whenever he sees barbecues, he is reminded of his childhood when it was called poverty to cook that way. With no electricity they had to rely on candles and lanterns fed by paraffin. In the evenings the women would sit on chairs in their doorways, either knitting crocheting or preparing food for the next day. Whilst playing games, the men would be talking, smoking and drinking wine and beer. Often Arthur would help grind coffee beans on a hand-operated grinder.

It was at La Linea that Arthur began to develop as a 'listener'. The entertainment often included tarot, teacup, sand or coffee-ground readings as well as other, more simple forms of divination. Though illiterate, his grandmother was very wise and, like other members of the family, was very psychic. She would show him the tarot and say, 'Look at the pictures as if you were reading a story like a comic.' Immediately Arthur was fascinated by the mystical, magical feeling that emanated from the cards. When his grandmother gave a tarot reading she naturally spoke all she saw, but Arthur would look at the cards to see where the words were printed. He quickly grasped that she was reading the cards intuitively and his listening powers became stronger as he heeded to what his grandmother said.

Once a week she would go with Arthur and some of her neighbours to another part of La Linea to visit a trance medium called La Patera. She frightened Arthur because on one hand she had only a thumb and two fingers. She was illiterate but under trance she could write poetry. Those who visited La Patera did not pay her with money but would bring flowers, food or some home-made article for the household. They would all gather round in a circle, the only light coming from candles. The medium would go into trance bringing forth a deep, manly voice. When addressing his grandmother, with Arthur sitting at her feet, the medium would say: 'Your grandson will go to England to live.' This unsettled him and he would implore his grandmother not to let La Patera send him to England. He does not remember anything else she said, only that this highly respected lady's prediction did come true.

One of Arthur's father's uncles, Benito Cano, once had a very frightening experience. He was a kindly man who enjoyed meeting friends at the local café or wine bar. Whilst drinking his morning coffee on one occasion he went into a coma. By the time he was taken to the hospital and examined, the doctor declared him dead on arrival. In Gibraltar when someone dies and there are no suspicious circumstances they are buried the next day. When the cortège reached its destination and the coffin was about to be lowered into the grave, Benito came out of his coma and realising he was in a box started kicking and banging with his hands until the coffin was opened. He was later declared alive by a doctor but died of a heart attack a few months later. Arthur is sure his great-uncle is around and that he helps him when he needs to find a way out of a 'boxed' situation.

Arthur's mother always did her shopping on a Wednesday when they would take the opportunity to visit Arthur's grandmother, Cristobalina Rio Roja, in Spain, because meat and vegetables were cheaper in La Linea than Gibraltar. His father used to bring little bars of lead from the dockyard which his mother would smuggle across the border. She would put these bars, the size of a small chocolate bar, in his sister's coat pockets, because children were not searched, only the adults. His sister would stand in the corner of the customs room and shake all over with fear. This made Arthur smile because, at the time, he knew nothing about the contraband. He was never allowed to smuggle because, had the border police ever asked him a question, he would certainly have 'spilled the beans', or in this case the lead bars. They were sold at a merchant's yard which helped buy some of the week's food. To this day he can still see his poor sister white with fright and shaking like an aspen.

When electricity was introduced to Arthur's grandmother's home it was a strange affair as there was just one power point in the middle of the ceiling from which hung a light bulb. It had two extensions, one for a wireless and the other for an electric iron. It was quite a relief for grandmother who had previously heated heavy irons on a charcoal stove.

As a child he was, by his own admission, 'stupidly obedient' and always did as he was told. He kept himself clean and tidy, only had two pairs of trousers and was told if he got his clothes dirty he would not be allowed to go to church or school! Whenever grandmother had to go out on an errand and could not take him with her she would leave him by the switched-on radio so he could hear the music. She told him that on her return she would want to know the exact time when the little bull came out from behind the coloured glass on the radio. Of course it never did; it was just her way of ensuring Arthur would listen and behave. The enforced radio listening was not without its good effects. The diet of not only music but plays and discussions helped him to grow in awareness and understanding.

Because he was a delicate child, Arthur was never allowed to play with other children. There were many cripples and beggars around so it was not considered safe. He had to be content playing with animals and he claims he learnt a lot by listening to them too. He now realises, as many of us do, that animals are also sensitive and have their own way of transmitting thoughts and feelings.

On one occasion whilst sitting in a café with his grandmother and parents, he saw three beggar boys fighting over a banana skin. They came over and asked for money. Arthur, afraid and shy, would not speak to them, whereupon his grandmother got angry and said: 'These are God's children too, so when they speak, you answer them. The only difference is that you don't ask them home to tea.' This was one of the first lessons she taught him about communication with other human beings. Something he would very much have to deal with in later years.

When Arthur left his grandmother's house in Spain to return home to Gibraltar he was surprised to find a baby brother had arrived during his absence. He also discovered his mother had taken in two cats belonging to a lady who had lived in the downstairs apartment. The female cat was called Minina and the kitten Horrore, meaning 'horror', so named because one of the cat-hating neighbours had poured a kettle of hot water over the animal and it was left looking rather odd. During the eighth month of her pregnancy, his mother had had a shock. In the middle of the night she was awakened by a lot of mewing and found that Minina had given birth to six kittens in Arthur's old cot which was right next to her bed. The shock must have been imprinted on her mind and when Arthur's brother was born he had a birthmark at the base of his spine which looked like the silhouette of a cat in a sitting position, with a curved tail. His mother and most of the family were superstitious, and although it could just have been a coincidence, it was certainly unusual and to them significant.

Arthur did not like school and his memories of schooldays in Gibraltar are very limited. One memory, however, stands out and concerned the time when an ammunition ship blew up in the harbour. At the time, Arthur and his classmates were sitting at their desks with hands clasped in prayer. Suddenly, everything around them shook from the explosion. Some of the children were cut by flying glass, while the teacher, Miss Parodi, fell down. All the children, except Arthur, ran to help her. He remained in the prayer position at his desk giving the impression of being the one with faith, which example helped the good lady to pull herself together and find the courage and faith to carry on herself. Later she complimented him on his behaviour; he did not dare tell her he wasn't courageous at all but frozen to the spot with fear. His mother, sister and brother escaped the explosion without injury but his father, a very keen fisherman, was out in his boat that day and reading one of his favourite cowboy books by Zane Grey whilst waiting for the fish to bite. He was blown overboard and suffered two ruptured eardrums that left him partially deaf.

From his first school he went on to an all-boys school where he formed a great friendship with two other boys named George Linares and Regelio Belotti. They would often go into Gibraltar's Roman Catholic cathedral, St Mary the Crowned, where in a cool spot behind the main altar they would play marbles. Their fun extended to flicking marbles against the carved stone panels, which make a great sound. The excitement soon ended once they were discovered by a priest. One wonders if he had the sense of humour to realise they were just boys being boys. Today Arthur still gets a kick out of doing things he should not. His sense of humour is no doubt keener than most, causing him to laugh at things others would not consider funny. He has an independent and strong personality and the more I know about Arthur the more apparent it becomes he will always go his own way.

The cathedral is full of his family's history. His father's parents were married there and their children christened and confirmed there, not to mention all the family funeral services. Arthur's sense of the ridiculous is aptly illustrated by his story of his father's and father's brother Jaime's First Communion. The ceremony lasted so long that both boys wanted to empty their bladders and went outside to the little courtyard wherein stands the shrine of Our Lady of Lourdes. Conveniently, there was a palm tree in a little white pot in the courtyard, so while everyone else knelt down to pray the two Molinary boys watered the palm tree.

In the early days he had to spend a lot of time in the cathedral with his godmother, Mrs Herminia Alicio. It was there he did a lot of praying and listening in what one might call a 'holy' atmosphere. He had to attend Mass and other services, which strengthened his desire to become a priest. He still retains a religious attitude but only in the sense of holding to his beliefs and expressing what he feels, but out of the 'cloth'. I sometimes tease Arthur about how he looks like a priest but certainly doesn't sound like one! To tell him he is setting a good example to others makes him smile but he insists he does as he feels he should and leaves others to judge the results. Which is as it should be.

Interesting to note is that in his childhood Arthur usually went to church on Sundays and holy days of obligation whilst the rest of the family attended only for weddings and funerals. He always felt better after morning Mass. This, however, had nothing to do with religion in the orthodox sense. He loved to listen and to feel the energy and aura inside the church building.

Having been brought up in the Church of England I often found a great power and peace and tranquillity in its buildings, even though it was hard for me to believe in what was going on. This applies to the holy places of any religion. Cathedrals, synagogues, mosques and temples are steeped in history and contain the beliefs and love that are practised there and to which people always respond as a creative force.

In spring 1954 Arthur swam into an oil slick in the Mediterranean Sea. He developed a bad eye infection which

17

meant that he had to attend hospital twice a day for treatment. His eyes developed a great sensitivity to light, a condition known as photophobia. Often at night he would rest his head on the window ledge and look out at the sunsets. He found this was the best time for 'Arturo' to talk to Arthur. Arturo is the name he gives to his inner voice, the one that tells him things he wouldn't otherwise know. Eventually, as he spoke only Spanish at this point in his life, he realised that, in effect, someone else was talking to him in English.

This was the start of the listener 'hearing'. It would always start by reliving and remembering the day's events, but then his mind would go into conversation mode and it was as if he could hear himself talking. Laying in bed looking at the colours of the evening sky, he would become completely absorbed. He realised that, although he could hear his own voice, his mouth was not moving.

The first time this occurred was, Arthur admits, the most frightening experience in his psychic career. He was, as ususal, lying down looking out of his bedroom window, when he suddenly became aware of a man standing as though behind his head. The man started speaking to him in English, a language he did not then understand. He could feel the man's warm breath on the back of his neck and he cried out in alarm, calling for his parents. They came rushing in to see what was wrong. Arthur implored them to tell the man to go away and leave him alone. They looked under the bed and anywhere a man could possibly be hiding but found no one. In those days when the fleets were in port, sailors would get drunk and break into houses looking for a good time. Or they would climb over locked gates and use the toilet. Arthur's father thought it must be an English sailor who had broken in, especially as Arthur said the man was dressed in white just like a sailor.

Later Arthur realised it was not a sailor he had sensed but someone who in psychic circles would be called a guide.

He prefers, however, to call him a friend from the unseen world. He still sees him and after that first meeting he continued his nightly meeting with the sunsets, moon and stars, and with the man. Sometimes he would get uncomfortable and frightened when he felt the breath and vibration of the man's voice on the back of his head. He would then tell him to go away, which he did. Eventually, though, Arthur overcame his fears and the man's quiet gentle voice would make him feel his heart had slowed down and was about to stop which gave him a beautiful sensation of peace.

Arthur is a natural psychic, born with a gift that can be expressed in many different forms. It does not always happen like this and although I was told I was born with the gift, it was twenty-five years before my psychic ability became apparent. There are no experiences I can recall before this happened but my 'awakening' to my ability was sudden and complete, when I became interested in the psychic and the development as though a switch had been pulled. It doesn't happen like that for everybody; we all get where we are meant to be and do what we have to but presumably only when we are ready for it. Arthur was born with this ability and has proved he is meant to be one of the finest mediums of this age.

# 3

## Good Advice from Anna Neagle

During the 1950s things were hard in Gibraltar and his father found it difficult to feed and clothe a family of five, so, on the suggestion of Arthur's godmother, Mrs Alecio, it was decided in 1954 that the family would emigrate to England. In November of that year the Molinary family – comprising Arthur, his parents, sister Jeronima and brother Mario – undertook the journey. Arthur's grandmother had wanted Arthur to stay in La Linea but it was decided the whole family should stay together.

They sailed on a liner called the *Orcades*, which to them was a great luxury. When the ship hit rough seas Arthur was very seasick. He remembers a steward saying to his father, 'Don't worry, I'll get something for the boy', and came back with some cream crackers on a plate. It reminded Arthur of the time his Aunt Mercedes, who ran a greengrocery shop in Gibraltar, had visited him and left a packet of Jacob's Cream Crackers by his bed. He was expecting sweets or chocolates or even custard creams, so could not understand why she had left him this strange gift. At this point in time, however, they settled his stomach and he developed a fondness for them that remains to this day.

On a very cold and foggy morning they arrived at Tilbury Docks on the Thames and he couldn't help remembering how his beloved grandmother had told them the sun never shone in England. When she had taken him on his first-ever visit to the cinema, which was in the open air, they had seen an English film (dubbed into Spanish) called *Footsteps in the Fog*. It was set in Victorian times and showed a London swathed in a perpetual blanket of fog. Now at Tilbury the foggy vista reached as far as the eye could see and Arthur's spirits sank.

They were met by his father's sister, Hermina, and they boarded the train to a place called Sawbridgeworth where she lived and where they would stay until things were sorted out. By the time they arrived, much to the relief of the whole family, the sun was shining, though with a crispness in the air that made them glad to see an English coal fire. Arthur felt he could sit and watch the flames for hours, no doubt seeing things in the ever-changing flames as many psychics do.

Sawbridgeworth was a very quiet village. During the war many children had been evacuated there, which made things more lively and interesting for Arthur. He soon made friends, one of whom was Anthony Newley who later became a famous actor, singer and songwriter. They had fun playing with a discus in the local meadow but enjoyed themselves even more so by using dried cowpats instead of the disc. They did, Arthur says, what young boys usually do, which leaves a lot to the imagination. Arthur can be quite secretive and has never said exactly what mischief they got up to.

School was not a joy for Arthur who, of course, still did not understand the English language too well. Nonetheless, he has some good memories and, being very obedient with a 'face teachers could trust', he was made a dinner prefect. Something which meant extra-large helpings of dessert, something he still enjoys. When exploring the locality with a cousin and friends he found a lot of satisfaction listening to a little pocket transistor radio. They would listen to pop music and all sorts of adventure programmes. It proved a good way for him to improve his English and learn about the English way of life. It gave him more practice in listening, too.

Sometime later his father decided they would all move to Fulham in London where he could get a better job. In 1956 he bought a house there and to everyone's delight they found themselves in a Gibraltarian and Spanish community. It was like home from home and there was more to do, though at times it was a little hard. The family was short of blankets and curtains and were forced to sleep on the floor as they had mattresses but no beds. They did have a small dinner table but only four chairs. His father placed a plank between two of the chairs so all five could sit down to meals. Arthur often had to push an old perambulator to the local gasworks bunker in order to buy two sacks of coke He was happy about this because his father gave him half a crown (12½ pence) pocket money each week which he saved to buy gramophone records. Which meant more listening.

Music has always played a great part in Arthur's life and always will. He has many favourite singers, of which by far the best, in his estimation, is Connie Francis. He was 'hooked on her' after his sister bought him a recording of her singing 'Who's Sorry Now'. He has a huge collection of her recordings and never tires of listening to them. Her music may drive some of us mad, but not him. He claims he gets something from her voice which is uplifting and calming. There is obviously a 'spiritual' link for him. Most of us find the same thing in music, art and theatre, among other creative interests. Everything with a sensitive vibration is a form of communication. In order to understand others we need to be able to experience whatever is necessary for us to be able to identify with them.

His memories of school in Fulham are almost nil. He can completely shut out things he doesn't like, something not all of us can do. It is, however, a very useful faculty for psychics, who, when dealing with people during readings, hear a lot of important things at the time but which are best not retained. This faculty is something I envy as it is not always easy to empty one's mind.

23

As money was scarce and the family needed extra funds his mother took a cleaning job in a small private hotel. The manageress asked her if, apart from the job, she could put in a couple of hours on a Saturday morning for a friend of hers who usually went away to a country cottage for weekends. His mother agreed and on her first visit to the rambling three-storey house, took Arthur along. She was nervous about having the responsibility of holding the keys to the house of wealthy people. She bought Arthur a copy of the *Eagle* and on arrival sat him at the end of a table in the dining room, where he could read it. Engrossed in his comic, he suddenly became aware of a lady coming into the room. 'I'll wait down here until your mother finishes upstairs,' she told him and went to sit at the furthest point of the room. As she walked past him she asked him what he was reading and when he told her she handed him a thin dark-blue book from the top of the piano, saying, 'Wouldn't you like to read to me instead?' As she sat down on the settee he noticed two teddy bears and a rag doll resting beside her. Looking straight at him, she added: 'Speak clearly as I want Sarah, mother bear and baby bear to hear you.' She even told them not to fidget as Arthur was going to read to them. Arthur must have stumbled a little, for eventually she came over to him and asked him whether he would like her to teach him to read. He agreed and over the following two months he got to know the lady well and all about her cuddly toys.

The lady turned out to be Anna Neagle, the famous actress, and in those few weeks she taught him more than any of his other teachers put together. She showed patience, care and understanding and never missed any of his mistakes, making him go back and read it all over again. She also told him that 'Whenever you stand up in front of people, the public, think of them as a patch of cabbages, and you will have no nerves.' This proved sage advice, although at the time, of course, he did not know he would eventually do public work in Spiritualist churches. One can only wonder what audiences would think of being seen as green cabbages!

In 1958 Arthur began to attend the Ackerman Secondary Boys School in Fulham. One of the only memories he has of that time is how his 'honest face' caused the headmaster to trust him in taking the school-dinner money to the bank every Friday. He enjoyed the walk and treated it as a sort of escape. He still often gets the same desire to get away for a time so that he can retreat into his own thoughts.

Every Friday afternoon there was a 'free will' lesson at school, when pupils could choose what to do from a number of things. Arthur chose a bookbinding class, and it was here that he discovered how much he loved creating things out of paper and putting them together to form a pamphlet or book. Consequently when he left school aged fifteen his first job was as an apprentice bookbinder. He soon found himself going to school again as he was required to learn his trade properly. He was happy to discover, however, that the Camberwell School of Arts and Crafts in south-east London was the first school he found enjoyable. In fact he loved it, and he shone in his craft. He made friends among the other students but there was one in particular, Tony Boyns, and they helped each other to prepare for their City and Guilds examination, which they passed. Some of his work was displayed at the National Book League, which was a great honour.

I stress the importance of Arthur's early life because it shows his great sensitivity and awareness, enabling him to find himself through his creative force and eventually his true vocation. Not that one can say that, even now, he has reached his goal, as it is possible he will go on to do even more advanced things.

It was around this time that Arthur felt the need to find out more about the afterlife. He overcame his shyness and began to visit places such as the Marylebone Spiritualist

Association, the Spiritualist Association of Great Britain and the London Spiritual Mission, not to mention many other Spiritualist churches and meeting places where he could witness psychic demonstrations. He found that by watching and listening to the 'old-time greats' he could learn a lot about how and how not to do it. His favourite medium was Nora Blackwood, whose outstanding work always inspired him. It was from the platform that she gave him his one and only message. Just a brief communication from his grandfather, Arturo, who told him that one day he would be standing where Nora was. It was a prediction that took fifteen years to materialise.

Arthur's connection with Nora intrigues me, as I first started my own psychic career under her tuition when I was persuaded to join her class. As in Arthur's case, she told me from the platform of the little church where she was demonstrating, that eventually I would stand where she was and that it would be when the Michaelmas daisies were in bloom. Six months later I did my first demonstration in that same church, surrounded by those flowers. By then Nora had gone on to greater things. She was also my favourite medium and one of the very best I have ever known. This is just one of the many parallels between Arthur and myself. I, too, went to many Spiritualist churches and meeting places to see how it all worked, thinking about what I would and wouldn't do if I ever became a medium. You can say the two of us were on the same wavelength, which was perhaps why we were drawn together in the first place.

In order to swell his weekly income and to further overcome his shyness, Arthur got himself a job as a waiter at the White City Greyhound Stadium in London. He was soon promoted to royal commis waiter and while working in the royal enclosure got to serve many celebrities, including Diana Dors, Bette Davis, Vera Lynn, Tom Jones, Roger Moore, Frances Day, Hattie Jacques, Ann Todd and David Frost, as well as, of course, the Queen and other royals. This might suggest Arthur is boastful and star-struck but I've found he treats everyone the same and enjoys meeting people whatever their station in life. He certainly made jokes and laughed with these people, which no doubt helped him to become the right person for the work he now does. I have seen him many times talk to and tease cashiers at the check-out in superstores and with almost anyone anywhere. I envy him this gift, especially as he makes the most miserable people laugh and respond positively to him. He truly sees and treats everyone on the same level.

Whilst working at White City Stadium Arthur served Diana Dors. At that time he had no knowledge of her interest in the psychic or that she had consulted Doris Stokes the well-known medium. Diana was one of his favourite stars and although as a waiter he was forbidden to speak to the diners or ask for their autograph, he couldn't resist asking her. The only reaction she made was a little smile and signal for him to wait. After a while she went to the ladies' room and returned with a black lace garter which she quietly slipped into Arthur's hand with a knowing wink. One of her typically generous gestures and to this day he still treasures it as a memory of a beautiful lady and a favourite star.

Personal relations often suffer with the demands of mediumship and though divorced, he is very proud of his son Roland, daughter-in-law Ruth and his three granddaughters Hazel, Heather and Emma, with whom he keeps as much contact as he can in his busy schedule.

Arthur was amused when Heather asked him, 'Grandad, those dead people you speak to, have they been buried?'

Successful relationships usually have to be with someone who is sympathetic to the subject and situation.

It was whilst working at White City that Arthur met a lady called Georgina Short. She had taken a washing-up job there to keep her mind occupied after the loss of her husband

and to get her out of the house. She had the most beautiful reddish-gold hair, with the saddest green eyes, and he could sense the heaviness in her heart. She told him her husband, Fred, had developed kidney disease and died as a result of it. Both were interested in the afterlife: it was a meeting of like minds that started a friendship of great depth and quality.

It was a beautiful day when they had their first date. They agreed to meet at a certain exit from Leicester Square underground station but at first neither could find the right one, much to their hilarity. It set the scene for a lovely day during which they saw the film *Dr Zhivago* and fell in love with its haunting theme song, 'Somewhere My Love'. This became a treasured memory and was to prove extremely important for Arthur. Gina, as she was normally called, suffered from leukaemia. They made a secret pact that whoever died first would try through an outside medium to sing that song to the other. She eventually died in 1976 at a time when Arthur was closely involved with the London Spiritual Mission.

At one of the meetings, a medium, Anne Archer, gave Arthur a message. She asked if he knew a lady who loved the colour red and would often wear it. Gina had reddish hair and always wore a lot of red clothes. She went on to ask him: 'Would it make sense to you if I sang the song from *Zhivago*? (Gina always referred to the film as just *Zhivago*.) The medium then started singing: 'Someday we'll meet again, my love; whenever the spring breaks through, you'll come to me out of long ago.' Those words meant everything to Arthur as their relationship was full of beautiful moments and many love songs. Thus Gina had fulfilled their pact.

Before her death, Gina and Arthur often organised meetings at Gina's home in order to help others by inviting mediums to give group readings. They provided a lot of evidence for those lucky enough to be present. One often learns more by

28

listening to others, and these groups provided Arthur with more opportunities to study and assimilate the experience of other mediums. Gina's late husband, Fred, was always present at these meetings communicating with Gina and Arthur.

When she was feeling well Gina had a great love of life and they enjoyed many happy experiences together. Arthur recalls that in one of their group meetings one lady would always go on the morning of the day to visit her husband's grave at the cemetery and place red roses on it. She would mentally ask him to come along to the group and pass comments about the flowers via the visiting medium. So every week the medium, whoever it was, would say to her: 'Your husband thanks you for the beautiful red roses you put on his grave.' At one of the meetings the medium said to the lady: 'Your husband is thanking you for the beautiful bunch of daffodils you placed on his grave.' Naturally the rest of the group were surprised and thought the medium had got it wrong. The meeting was taken by a Mrs Swan, a notably strict and somewhat tough medium who always did her best to give words of comfort. After the meeting the old lady told Mrs Swan that she always bought her husband half a dozen red roses every week but on this occasion she could not afford them so bought a bunch of daffodils instead.

On another occasion a friend of Gina's called Vera came along to one of the meetings. Vera's mother had recently died. The medium for the evening was Mrs Rose Brugier who worked in trance and had a guide, a French Sister of Mercy. She gave messages to everyone present but left Vera until last. She then started by telling Vera: 'My dear, I have to vacuum your carpet; all this white dust everywhere, your poor mother isn't going to rest until you have cleared all the powder.' She then continued to give excellent evidence of Vera's mother, with a description of her character, likes and dislikes, and her final illness. After the meeting Vera started telling them all about how much her husband Bob

29

disliked her mother and she him. In her will she had wished to be cremated and the ashes scattered into the Grand Union Canal. When it came to the day Vera had arranged to do this she came down with a heavy cold and could not go so she asked her husband if he would be so kind as to take Mum to the canal. Although he disliked his mother-in-law, he agreed to do it.

Bob and their pet dog got into the car and drove off, but instead of going straight to the canal, he stopped off at the pub and had a few beers. When it was time to go home, he got into the car with the dog and suddenly realised his mother-in-law was still there waiting to be dumped into the canal. By this time he could not be bothered and when he got out of the car with the dog to relieve himself, he decided to scatter the ashes over a bush. As he did so he failed to notice the dog was under the bush, and with a feeling of satisfaction they went home where Bob sat in front of the fire and went to sleep. When Vera got out of bed to get a drink she popped into the drawing room and saw her husband and the dog fast asleep. The dog was covered in white powder and so was the carpet. Vera let out a scream, waking up man and dog, and the dog shook itself, scattering more white powder everywhere. When she asked Bob what he had done with her mother, he just didn't have an answer.

Arthur learned a lot about mediumship and how it functions through these groups – every medium, he discovered, has his or her own individual way of working.

When Arthur's grandmother died of old age at 102, the family were able to get her a place very near to 'grandad's green nylon socks'! In Spain not all corpses are buried in the ground; some are placed in a wall that looks a bit like an apartment block. The coffins are put into a niche in the wall and sealed with a marble slab with details of the deceased engraved upon it. The families then place flowers and photos outside the slab. When his grandfather, Salvador, died the only niche available was right at the top. It made it very awkward for his grandmother, who, when she went to visit the family graves every Sunday, would have had to have climbed up a ladder to reach it. Fortunately, an aunt carried out this difficult chore for her.

Eventually a new block was built and the family clubbed together and bought a space for Grandad on the ground level so Grandmother could pray and talk to him in comfort. Whenever a coffin is moved from one place to another, a member of the family has to be present to witness the re-opening. Arthur's Aunt Carmen volunteered but when the coffin was opened all she could see was dust. At the end where the feet should have been, all that remained was a pair of green nylon socks! No one ever told Arthur's grandmother how much was paid to get her closer to Grandad's green nylon socks, but it made her happy so they considered it worthwhile.

Other deaths of those dear to him have profoundly impacted on his life. His father died in 1984 aged seventy-three. A few weeks before his death, Arthur's father was on heavy medication which gave him hallucinations. Whilst Arthur and his mother were sitting by his bed and talking about food his father suddenly pointed up to the top of the wardrobe and said, 'Look, Cecilia, my uncle Laureno is sitting on top of the wardrobe.' Mother, as calm as ever, asked him, 'Do you want the rice or mashed potatoes?', before adding in a matter-of-fact sort of way, 'He's your uncle, tell him to get down.'

The loss of her husband affected his mother greatly as they were a close and devoted couple and she missed him. She suffered a stroke in April 1985 and Arthur left his job in order to nurse her. When she suffered another stroke soon after she was taken to live with her daughter as she needed a woman's care twenty-four hours a day. It was at around this time that Arthur first met me and, encouraged by me, took his first steps in his psychic career.

# 4

## *Wendy: A Testimonial*

Arthur often recalls the training I have given him and how happy he was, and is, to have been introduced to the College of Psychic Studies. To me it gives one the satisfaction of knowing one has passed on one's knowledge and experience to others. If they listen and try out what they learn, it is possible to achieve their full potential. Arthur has 'found' himself by trying many and varied things – different kinds of divination that in the end all add up to the same thing, but cater for those who respond more readily to the apparently 'magical and mysterious'. I am proud to have been instrumental in bringing to notice one who has an exceptional gift and who will, I have no doubt, go further yet. If we had not met, I am certain Arthur would have found another way through, although I believe most things are preordained and he was sent to the one who could help him best.

In many senses Arthur is a very private person. He often says that 'my favourite space is that room hidden somewhere in my mind where I sit, wait and listen.' We enter our own private space where only the invited few may enter; we create the conditions needed to regenerate, to help us function as we like to and put ourselves in a good frame of mind. Arthur keeps out all colours and noises that do not create harmony, and surrounds himself with furnishings he likes, with favourite photographs, pictures and, most importantly, music. In his 'quiet room' he tries to keep out all those things which are foreign to his nature. It is here where he waits for those he has loved to come and visit. This is the reason why when working at the College of Psychic Studies or in other people's homes, mediums, psychics and healers cannot do more than the conditions generated will permit.

Every medium has their strengths and weaknesses. Arthur feels that having one's future told doesn't necessarily help one to meet it. He considers his main strength is to comfort those who mourn and help guide their future. He thinks of himself as a candle and tries to relight a flame within those who come to see him.

There are many testimonials to Arthur's work as a medium whose glowing terms bear witness to the wonderful evidence and comfort he has given. One example, given to me by Wendy Crane from Manchester, is worth examining at some length.

Mrs Crane wrote: 'I first went to the CPS (College of Psychic Studies) for a reading with Arthur Molinary after the death of my daughter aged twenty. It was the first time I ever consulted a medium or practitioner of any sort, or even considered doing such a thing.' She went on to say she was aware that some people think that mediums profit from the vulnerable, the weak and the bereaved. She had her own ideas but was far from being vulnerable to any 'crazy manipulator'. She found Arthur to be 'reassuringly sane' and with 'both feet on the ground'. She approached her interview with an open mind and was honest enough to tell him she was a drowning person clutching at a straw and that she thought Arthur had as much chance of getting her to dry land as that straw. Arthur offered to tape-record the reading, which she immediately accepted as she would then have a permanent record to listen to again and again. If there were any doubts about the medium and what took place, she could then prove them to be right or wrong. Fortunately there was no need to worry, despite the feeling she would not receive anything of value, since in the first few moments of her reading she became convinced the information was not coming by normal means.

Her husband, a normal and rational man, had not wanted Wendy to see Arthur as he feared she would come away disappointed and upset. After hearing the tape of that first reading he was totally certain Arthur had communicated with their dead daughter, Abigail. Arthur was not told of the connection when the husband saw him for a reading but he felt he had connected with the same young lady before.

During a series of readings which both husband and wife attended they were convinced that the picture given of Abigail's complex personality was complete and consistent. Arthur saw her as 'beautiful and open with a fresh childlike face, a small body, a little woman who hated putting on weight and hating herself. With a direct gaze, a sense of humour lightening up the room, determination, a love of life's pleasures, very bright and having everything to live for'. All these things, together with other details, were true and Wendy said they were a long way from the generalised stereotype of a twenty-year-old that one might make up if one was simply guessing.

During the first interview Arthur did not at first mention Wendy's son, but later having described her mother and mother-in-law, who were with Abigail, he said: 'All three women will be helping the three of you – you, your husband and who is the third?' Wendy, breaking her own rule of not feeding information, told Arthur it was her son. He made no further reference to it until the end of the reading when he assured Wendy that Abigail would be helping them all, and specifically her son, to communicate better. Despite it being the only reference to her son in the first reading, it was very meaningful. They had as a family often talked about the son's lack of communication skills. Abigail had been quite concerned about this. In the week before she died it had been mentioned in the context of his intention of staying in academia and his consequent need to improve his teaching skills. Significantly, Abigail was a natural teacher, patient and intuitive in recognising problems and imaginative in supplying answers.

During the second reading Arthur returned to the theme of Abigail's concern for her brother. He said: 'She is with you all the time, especially your son, like a guardian angel. She fought her brother's battles for him when she was alive and is still fighting. She is like a kind of "agony aunt". They were very close and he is still grieving. She is worried about her brother's blood pressure and says he should not be suffering from this condition at his age.' Then he added: 'He loses control!' This was true as the son had confessed to Wendy his blood pressure was, according to the university doctors, higher than it should be, as he was overweight. She admitted her son lost his temper in a spectacular way when he was upset by something, to a point where he hyperventilated. Abigail had mentioned her concern about this a few days before she died.

Wendy was very impressed by Arthur's psychic ability. She had been aware of how some psychics feed back snippets of information but do not create the feeling of the presence of the loved one. Arthur did, however, create the feeling of the comunicator's invisible presence in the room, and to Wendy and others it underpinned and strengthened the evidence for the continuation of life.

Wendy felt Arthur's account of what she and her husband did on finding Abigail dead to be remarkable. The evidence was spread over two readings for her and her husband. They felt Arthur had provided a genuine link with Abigail because it contained elements which he could not understand or make sense of. In the first reading Arthur said: 'She is saying when she was dead you touched her body...' He stopped abruptly here. 'You touched her face, kissed her all over like this.' He gestured kissing her eyes, nose, mouth, cheeks and chin. Wendy acknowledged this was true. It was something she did when Abigail was alive as well as just after she died. The ritual way in which she kissed Abigail is not a common gesture and surely could not be guessed.

Interestingly, Wendy felt the abrupt stop after the word 'body' seemed to reflect something she did before kissing Abigail's face. In needing to say goodbye and to touch a part of her that was relatively warm (rigor mortis was rapidly setting in), she touched the front part of Abigail's body, including her breasts, which had become exposed. She then lifted the elastic of the leggings Abigail was wearing and touched her stomach. She then felt she was invading her privacy. In life they would not have been inhibited by each other's nakedness. Wendy felt that Arthur had, by stopping after the word 'body', given evidence of something deeply personal between the two women.

More evidence came when Arthur told Wendy she did something with Abigail's lips. Here he gestured with his own mouth by squeezing his lips with his fingers to produce a figure of eight. This immediately conjured up a picture of her daughter lying there. He said: 'You made like a figure-of-eight shape,' which was true. Then he added: 'It sounds almost kinky unless you know the circumstances.' When they found Abigail dead, Wendy and her husband tried to revive her. He told Wendy to breathe into Abigail's mouth but, owing to rigor mortis, her jaw was locked fast and she could not open it. She continued to try, this time in the presence of her son, and made the gesture Arthur so accurately described, drawing back Abigail's mouth so she could see her teeth. The lips were the only thing that could be moved.

Wendy thought Arthur sometimes misunderstood infor- mation that came through especially when he spoke of Abigail's fear of life itself. Abigail said it was nobody's fault but her own fears and phobias. She continued to repeat this despite Wendy's questions and feelings of guilt that she had been unable to help her daughter or give her what she needed. Finally Arthur said: 'She says Suzie did it. Suzie made her feel not confident and afraid of life.' This puzzled Wendy as she thought it contradicted what Arthur had been saying. She could not think of anyone called Suzie in Abigail's life and certainly no one who would have done such a thing.

Wendy was impressed by Arthur's confidence in what he said, although she felt he was misinterpreting something that caused her to fail to recognise a very creditable communication containing significant evidence. After reaching home Wendy eventually recalled that Suzie was one of the several names she had called her daughter as a child when they were playing a certain game. She then remembered using the name and playing the same game in the last few days before she died. Thus Suzie was Abigail herself and by saying 'Suzie did it' she was restating that she was the cause of her own fears. Wendy thought this was typical of Abigail's personality and quirky sense of humour, and that, frustrated by Wendy's failure to accept what she said, she used their game to convince her mother both of her continuing life beyond the physical and her admission of her own responsibility for what happened.

In one of her husband's readings Arthur conveyed a joke of Abigail's without even realising it was a joke, thus displaying his ability to give exactly what he gets but leaving it to the recipient of the message to interpret and understand. Arthur told him that Abigail was offering both of them (Mr Crane and Arthur) a glass of sparkling pink wine. Arthur assumed she must have enjoyed such wine and then accurately pinpointed dates of celebrations – her own and her brother's birthdays, and, poignantly, the New Year celebration that had been the last such shared family event before her death – when they had drunk together. Arthur felt she was letting them know that she would still be there, eating, drinking and being merry but no longer afraid of getting fat.

Wendy said her daughter did enjoy good food and wine. She got depressed if she put on weight although it was not because of food but due to some medication she had been given. However, what lifted the communication above something that might have been produced by any other good psychic was the underlying joke, which Arthur himself could not possibly pick up on. Both Abigail and her father were wine gourmets and both, on occasions, had been a little snooty about 'pink' sparkling wines. Moreover, Abigail had often teased her father by using the word 'pink' rather than the more correct 'rosé'. Wendy felt that Arthur had here captured the essence of the relationship between father and daughter.

Abigail's communication shows how a medium should work in order to avoid the ever-present danger of misinterpretation – the need to give what comes through as clearly as possible, but to let the recipient of the message accept what they know to be true. Too many psychics insist they know what they are talking about and refuse to allow the recipient to interpret the communication otherwise. Arthur Molinary, by contrast, is scrupulous in giving exactly what he gets, and in standing by what he says. In the end it will usually prove right, but only those on the receiving end can work that out.

Wendy said that, with Arthur, even when something simple like a word or phrase came through, there always seemed to be complications. One such instance occurred when Arthur was talking about some flowers that had seemingly no significance in relation to Abigail. However, the talk about flowers made her think of another flower that had been on her mind, though she couldn't quite remember its name. She did recall that, as a child, Abigail had liked its name when she saw it on a box of crayons – it was the name of a particular colour. This flower also grew in the family garden and seemed to be unusually abundant that season. Wendy asked Arthur its name and after listening carefully for a moment he told her that Abigail had said: 'It's a periwinkle, of course!' And then after listening again he said: '... And it's coming through the path!' mimicking the triumphant tone of whoever was talking to him. This was absolutely true – Wendy had been thinking of the flower and seeing it in her mind as she left home that morning. She asked Arthur what the periwinkle looked like but he had no idea until a little later he said: 'It looks like bluebells, blue.' Which is also true.

Wendy said some of Arthur's evidence concerned her ongoing day-to-day life and showed that a loved one who dies is still around, both in the home and wherever else we may be. A good example of this was when Arthur mentioned a bookcase to the left of Wendy's chair in the sitting room. In fact, the room was lined with bookshelves but there was one bureau bookcase which was the only thing Wendy actually thought of as a book*case*. Arthur then said: 'At eye level four along to the left there is a book to remind you of Abigail.'

The bookcase contained only three books which had a particular connection with Abigail and the one corresponding with Arthur's description was an edition of T.S. Elliot's *Cats*, given to Abigail by Wendy. Next to it was another edition of the same book given to Abigail by the family. Wendy said there were hundreds of books in that room. She thought it had to be more than coincidence that Arthur had chosen the right one, or that he really had been guided by Abigail who was now living in a different dimension.

# 5

## *The London Spiritual Mission*

Arthur gave his first public demonstration of clairvoyance at the London Spiritual Mission. The London Spiritual Mission is a Spiritualist church founded by Edward Beard in 1912 and is one of the most beautiful of all Spiritualist churches. The premises started life as a stable to house horses and carriages behind the imposing residences near Notting Hill, London. Upon entering the building one senses an aura of peace and tranquillity, helped along by two stained-glass windows dedicated to a great lady, Nan McKenzie, who served there and helped countless people with her wonderful healing work for many years. But the thing that strikes one most are the inscriptions on either side of a picture of Jesus which say 'Give out Light' and 'Give out Love'. Good advice to anyone of any race, colour or creed.

Arthur had been suddenly asked to stand in for a medium who had not turned up. With shaking legs and trembling voice he stood up to give his first message. Pointing to a pleasant-looking middle-aged man sitting near one of the stained-glass windows, he asked him if the name Rosemary meant anything to him. Whereupon the man stood up with angry face pushed his way through the people occupying the same pew and headed for the door. Before he left he turned and shouted at Arthur: 'It's a lie, it's a lie, I never touched her!' and then slammed the door behind him. It was a rather startling introduction to his public work, but at least he did

41

not need to go into detail as one name was enough to 'hit home'. One needs a sense of humour and often a very broad back in order to do good work, and Arthur is well equipped with both.

From that first demonstration he went from strength to strength, and in the subsequent years his reputation drew many 'celebrities' who came to consult him. Arthur has met the rich and famous, exchanged views with politicians, travelled with explorers, sailed with pirates, sung with some of the greatest singers of our time, bowed before kings and queens, prayed with saints and a string of sinners and murderers. He has travelled into space and over golden yesterdays and has flown into the future. He has laughed and cried at life's mysteries and acted with the best of actors. He says he has done this without moving a muscle.

A large majority of his clients are famous or very well-known people – even the stars need help and direction. He must hold the record for seeing so many celebrities and public figures over the years, and all by word of mouth as there has never been any need for him to advertise. Even Queen Elizabeth, the Queen Mother, sent her valet Leslie to see Arthur, with all sorts of questions. Barry, who was Prince Charles's secretary, came with questions about the Prince and Princess Diana. Lord and Lady Evelyn Delves Broughton received great help from him as did Prince Albert of Monaco, son of Princess Grace (formerly Grace Kelly) and Prince Rainier. It is always interesting to meet famous people 'in the flesh' so to speak, and it is good to discover they are only human and respond to Arthur's friendly but professional approach.

Amongst a very long list of names who have been for readings are Anthony Newley's daughter, Tara, and his mother, Grace; actresses Sian Phillips, Ann Todd, Joan Sims, Dulcie

Gray, Shirley Eaton, Frances Day, Virginia McKenna, Meera Syall, Jerry Hall, Linda Robson, Amanda Burton and the renowned singer Georgia Brown; actors Alec Pettyfer and Paul Rhys; and pop stars Sinéad O'Connor, Geri Halliwell, Freddy Mercury and Dave Clark (of the famous Dave Clark Five), the latter becoming a good friend of his. Patrick Walker the famous astrologer has been, as has George Galloway, MP, TV producer Maurice Leonard and Nigel Hall, then head of Carlton TV.

Two of the celebrities who have come to Arthur were the son of the famous Scout leader Lord Baden Powell and his wife, who liked to be called simply Robert and Patience. Patience consulted Arthur over a period of twelve years, but Robert was also very interested and both kept tape recordings of their readings with Arthur.

During the first reading with Patience Arthur described a gentleman who stood like a stallion in the field, full of pride and dignity. He had a mindset just like a policeman's and was caring and understanding just like a father to his daughter. Patience's reply was that 'My father was the local village bobby.' When her mother communicated Arthur felt her character was 'one degree cooler than the weather', but she was nonetheless a good person. Patience once asked her mother if she could help 'Auntie' in this world, who had suffered several strokes, and the reply was that they were all happy and at peace 'over there'. Arthur got the distinct feeling that Auntie was not wanted yet. Patience replied: 'I'm not surprised as they didn't get on when they were together.' Which only goes to show that people do not necessarily change when they pass on.

When both Robert and Patience were concerned about moving and selling their small farm where they had several horses, her father told them they would move but would have to leave four horses behind; there would not be enough room in the new place, which was true. Then he said with the financial worries they were having he would not let them down. Things would change, even if it was at the eleventh hour; he would not see them put out on the streets. They would move in the tenth month, October. This happened as predicted four years later.

The interpretation of time is always a problem for mediums. Spiritualists believe the other world to be a timeless dimension where people lose the 'atmosphere' of the earthly world and have to adjust to a new existence. Because of their timeless existence our loved ones see everything on the same 'level' as if it is all happening now. It is as if they are seeing further ahead than we. This can make communication difficult to some extent but things we cannot immediately understand can come to pass later on.

On one occasion Patience was told by one of Robert's aunts called Heather (Arthur got her name quite clearly) that she had come to help Robert with his horses. He felt Heather had more time and love for horses than her fellow humans. She especially mentioned one of Robert's mares. Patience explained that one had been put out to stud and had become rather unwell. She was a little reluctant to tell Robert that Aunt Heather said the mare had a bladder infection. Arthur then explained to Patience he wasn't a healer but whenever he heard of people that he liked and cared about, even animals, who were ill, he always performed a mental routine. He would envisage a skating rink and then take them skating. In his mind he would hear music which helped him go off into a Torvill and Dean-type routine with his partner. He still insists he is not a healer but believes this kind of mental projection is purer than the laying-on-of-hands method. The recipient is not aware of anything coming their way so cannot create mental or emotional barriers but the transmitted energy reaches the patient, giving them a boost like taking a pill.

It is interesting to note that not all mediums are healers and do not claim to be. Those who do, like Arthur, have different methods and ideas. I personally believe in the words of the old song, 'It's not what you do but the way that you do it, that's what gets results'. In my long experience I have witnessed healers doing all sorts of strange things which others often criticise. I believe that any individual should do as they are impressed. As long as the heart is in what they do, the results should be good, and it is the results that count. So Arthur does it his way and it does work for him. So often Arthur comes up with some very strange ideas but which turn out to work. I have a lot of ideas different from Arthur's and can't criticise what he does because, like his, mine get results. Variety is the spice of life.

Patience also told Arthur one of her mares was very weak and had no appetite. He asked her for a photo of the mare and took the mare into his mental skating rink. We may as well laugh at this and be reminded of a Walt Disney cartoon. Arthur skated with the horse to a very peaceful melody and felt he was preparing her to meet her maker. Later Patience told him on the first evening after Arthur had sent the energy the mare became peaceful and there was a glow around her. She was the chief of Patience's herd and a few days later she saw her go to a younger mare and it looked like they were having a 'nose to nose' conversation. That night the older mare died and the next day the younger one had taken over as head of the herd. It would seem the older horse had prepared the younger one for new duties.

Patience had a problem with another horse whose back was affected so much a saddle could not be worn. Arthur took a friend of his to see Patience, a man called Jonathan Day, who was an excellent healer and dealt with horses with equine behavioural problems. Arthur was cautious about being near to horses, having had a previous bad experience. When Jonathan was ready to see the horses, he asked Arthur if he would like to watch, and not wishing to appear afraid, he agreed. As they neared the field where the horses were, Arthur became aware of an old mare called Triple Lily, who was then in the other world, walking behind him. It was the same mare with whom he had skated on his mental ice rink. He felt she was showing her thanks to him and was happy freely roaming the fields in another dimension.

Arthur began to smell 'stable odours' and as he got into his mental pictures he noticed one of the mares coming towards him as though she recognised him. She came very close and stood looking at him. He felt rather uneasy and suddenly all the other mares came forward and stood in order of dominance, as though Jonathan and Patience were not important. He nervously called out to Patience, asking if they were all going to charge him, but she told him the mare closest to him was Triple Day, the filly of Triple Lily, whom he had helped with healing. He felt very uncomfortable with all the horses staring at him and, as he walked back to the house, wondered if the filly could actually see her mother standing behind him. I believe that animals are very sensitive and do survive and that they have a soul like humans do, though obviously one suited to their situation.


When Diana Churchill saw Arthur at the College, his first vision was of Hollywood studio logos. He told her she either had connections with Los Angeles or the film industry. She told him both applied to her. He told him he saw a man walking towards him: in one hand he had a bottle of whisky and in the other hand a glass of the same. He said: 'This is your father,' to which she replied, 'It sounds like him.' In his mind Arthur was looking through an open door and seeing a lake where a boat with a fishing rod in it was moored. Her father was holding Arthur's arm and pushing him out of the door towards the boat. Asking Diana if this made sense she said, 'Yes, if my father had something to do he would push you out of the house whilst still talking to you.'

Arthur had no idea who her father was until he saw the whisky bottle and then realised it was the great Winston Churchill. When she asked him if he knew who her father was, he said 'yes' and then added, 'the government will get involved in Diana's death.' To which she replied, 'Why would they be interested in my death'? There was no explanation for this statement at the time but it could have been that Winston was forecasting Princess Diana's death, which happened a while later; they had family links. His daughter's closing comment was to ask: 'Had he met the little corporal?' – a reference, of course, to Adolf Hitler.

Sometimes communicators do not mention their actual names, but give another one that the sitter will recognise. Such was the case when Arthur could see lots of books around a gentleman client who told him he was a publisher of historical books for Penguin. The communicator was his father who had died from a heart attack. During the reading Arthur heard a very sexy lady's voice saying 'me Tondelayo', which reminded him of a film he had seen starring the beautiful actress Hedy Lamarr. The man said it was his stepmother. His father had been married to Hedy Lamarr, who played Tondelayo in one of her most celebrated film roles.


After Jean Percy Craven of West Sussex came to Arthur for a reading she described him as having a very special gift of healing with the unique ability to make whoever comes to him feel 'there is a light at the end of the tunnel', which earned him her gratitude. In the first reading he was able to describe her husband's last moments of pain before his passing. She felt it uncanny that a complete stranger could describe such a personal moment. Yet he had the compassion and depth of feeling that made her feel he had been there and understood.

Arthur later asked her why he felt he was in the middle of the Grand Canyon, to which she replied that she had spent most of her married life with her first husband, Salvador, in Arizona; the Grand Canyon was very much a part of their lives. He spoke of the joys of riding a donkey, something which Jean had done only once in her life whilst on their many travels. She felt that, although these things seemed small and even insignificant in themselves, by bringing them through Arthur helped her to resolve her sadness.

Jean considered Arthur always captured the essence of the departed person's personality, no matter who it was communicating. She felt that whenever Arthur sensed the presence of her loved ones they were more real to him than she was, sitting in front of him. He brought Salvador back into her life in a way she never felt possible. References to coffee with camel's milk, for instance, were a nice allusion to their days together in the Middle East. There were many very personal and even teasing references which were only applicable to her relationship with Salvador and could have no meaning to anyone else. Expressing her great admiration of his wonderful gift and the hard work it involves and his determination to be perfect in his work, she noted that he was able to pinpoint anniversaries such as birthdays and so on with great accuracy. She thought Arthur has a wonderful gift for healing a person's damaged aura, 'combing it out', as he says, in order to help the client sort out the problems they are facing. Sometimes Arthur's advice isn't for the faint-hearted but you can trust him to spell it out just as he sees it. If your world is full of deadbeats he is more than likely to tell you so, and if you don't choose to take his or the departed's advice then he will certainly repeat it on the next visit.

* * *

When Mrs Jean Webber entered into Arthur's room for a reading she appeared to be quite ordinary. She was not nervous but very quiet, not saying much and her replies to his statements were given in a very 'clipped' manner. There was nothing about her that could give any medium ideas as to her background and the fact that she was the mother of two of the best-known musical personalities of our day – Julian and Andrew Lloyd Webber. Arthur began by telling her she had four children, two of whom were lost in early childhood and two sons who had reached full manhood and were still in this world. He also sensed music all around her. He made contact with her husband, mother and father in the other world and his mention of German links was accepted by her. The only name given was Bill, which belonged to her husband who was never called William. She did not seem particularly interested in contacts and was obviously hoping for some more 'earthly' advice.

As he heard an organ playing, Arthur saw in his mind scenes from the 1940s film *Phantom of the Opera* in which a man in a mask was playing an organ. Jean said her husband, whom Arthur had called a reserved, unassuming man who never showed emotion for anything except music and would cry like a baby at times when dealing with music, played the organ and was very involved in music.* Later when Arthur told Jean he had a friend who used to play the organ in St George's Church, he asked her why she thought he was remembering this. She replied that her husband had also played the organ there. Her husband also loved travel, water and open spaces, as Arthur mentioned.

Jean's husband, Arthur told her, was trying to help his

---

*William Lloyd Webber (1914–82) was a respected composer in his own right.

49

youngest son who, Arthur thought, was called Jewel (it was actually Julian) and who, he said, had emotional troubles and a love of Oriental women and music. He suffered from black moods and would always have psychological problems. Jean's husband then said his eldest was like him, emotional and very much concerned with music. Arthur asked Jean if her son liked cats because he saw him surrounded by them and felt he would achieve lots of great projects. She replied that 'Andrew' liked animals but not cats, so she could not understand this. She had previously said she did not understand the *Phantom of the Opera* reference in connection with her husband playing the organ.

This is a perfect example of where a medium was getting significant messages which were inexplicable at the time but would later make sense. The impressions received were given before the musical shows *Phantom of the Opera* and *Cats* were probably composed and written. Certainly Jean Webber the mother of Andrew Lloyd Webber could not have known of them, so the medium could not have read her mind nor have obtained the information from anywhere or anyone else except her husband in the other world.

When Ellen Lancaster entered his room, Arthur immediately saw in his mind an MGM logo and heard Matt Monro singing 'Born Free'. Her main communicator was her son, whose name was Raj but which he had changed to Paul. He had been murdered. Arthur felt two blasts in his chest: Paul had been shot twice. He then described a white house with a verandah and garden. This was Paul's mother-in-law's house where the murder had taken place; his body was found in the road outside the house. Paul gave a description of the man who had shot him; he said he looked like Idi Amin, a good description of the mother-in-law's boyfriend. Arthur also saw Paul on top of some cliffs painting. His mother said he was a painter and loved to do beach scenes. In response to Arthur describing him as a Tarzan figure wearing only a tiny pair of shorts, Ellen said it was all he ever wore as it all took place in Kenya.

At the end of the session Arthur once again saw the MGM logo of a lion roaring and heard 'Born Free' but this time he also saw Ellen bending over from the back view displaying her rear. When asked if these things meant anything to her she replied: 'I have a few scars on my bottom from when I was attacked by a lion.' The song 'Born Free', of course, is about a lion.

Arthur recalls one lady who came for a reading though he cannot remember her name. She was an elderly lady of eighty-two, very well educated, nicely dressed and very Victorian. It looked as though she was wearing a stiff corset: when he asked her to sit in his very comfortable Queen Anne armchair she did so but remained very erect, not allowing herself to relax. He started to tune in to her life, situation and problems when suddenly he exclaimed: 'Madam, have I got this right? You have *three* husbands in the spirit world?' Her reaction to this was memorable: she leaned slightly forward and said: 'That's right, young man, but I don't want to talk to any of *those* bastards.' As the reading continued Arthur could see husband number four coming towards her. He decided not to tell her but thought, 'Good luck to her; while there's life, live it!'

Mary Martin from Middlesex had already been to the College for a few readings. When she met Arthur for the first time she was quite overwhelmed at his accuracy in describing loved ones who had passed on. In describing her mother he sensed she had been exhausted and confused, with bad breathing problems. It was as though her lungs were filling with fluid. Apparently the mother had been in a nursing home because of senility and died of pneumonia. He gave an amazing description of her personality and told Mary her mother was helping her to get the support she needed, as she knew what it was like not to get any, either morally or financially, as her husband hadn't given her any, and she was aware Mary hadn't anyone to support her.

Arthur mentioned the year of 1976, which was when her mother died. Of a family of four, Arthur said her mother was talking about the boy and two in the spirit world. Mary thought she could be referring to two grandsons, one of whom could be her son Andrew. Arthur then asked her if she had lost a son who, had he lived, would have been in his early twenties. Andrew was twenty-one at the time of his passing. Arthur described his nature and mannerisms with superb accuracy, as if he had known him all his life. With a mouthful of words he seemed to have brought Andrew into the room. So strong was his presence that, although Mary could not see him, she could feel him.

Arthur told her Andrew had died quickly, and he sensed a greyness in his aura which suggested one of two things: either confusion in his mind at the time of passing, or he had a hand in his own passing. He felt Andrew had been depressed the last six months of his life. As Mrs Martin revealed, Andrew had indeed been mentally ill for the last six months of his life prior to committing suicide.

It is interesting to note here that Arthur claims to be able to see the auras of people in both worlds. Although I personally cannot see or read auras, I have no doubt this is one of Arthur's faculties. When interpreting the aura it would appear the impressions come as unedited pictures, thrown up by the mind for the medium to make sense of. By contrast, with direct communication from the other side it would seem the spirits, using our memory bank as a dictionary, tend to do the editing for us, enabling the most accomplished of them to pass very accurate and specific information through the medium.

Arthur continued with Mary by saying he saw stripes on

Andrew's chest when he died. He was wearing a striped shirt. Arthur asked 'who drowned?' Tragically it was Andrew. Arthur felt Andrew didn't realise it was water, possibly because of his confused state of mind. He then asked if there was bitterness between Andrew and his father because the latter had said a lot of poisonous things that hurt his son badly and deeply. Mary said it was a true account of a man who bore the illness his son inherited. Then Arthur became puzzled because he said he had to talk to Robert. It was Andrew's father's name.

The son then conveyed his love of and rapport with music, and Arthur heard a song from the show *Cabaret*, particularly the line 'What good is sitting alone in your room?' Mary explained all of this was true as Andrew not only spent a lot of time alone is his room, but went off on long walks. They were safety valves for his frustration. She also said her son had left lots of unsolved puzzles and questions, just as Arthur felt was the case. In answer to Arthur saying Andrew was showing him a lot of coloured tickets which suggested he liked the theatre and was artistic, she said Andrew was extremely knowledgeable about music and played the piano extremely well. He had written a play and generally had great knowledge and appreciation of the arts. He had lectured on Russian authors whilst at public school, something, too, that Arthur sensed.

Andrew said he would be taking Mary to see some horses at Christmas. She thought this unusual as normally she had no interest in horses. Later, when she was spending Christmas with friends, they especially asked her to arrive in time to go and watch their daughter at her riding school. Also, Andrew told Mary 'she had still got that picture'. This was an artist's drawing of Andrew when he was fifteen. Arthur emphasised that Andrew had strong feelings about the picture. Whenever Andrew came home from school or Cambridge he would always say to Mary: 'I wish you would take that picture down.' By the manner in which Arthur expressed the message Mary felt it could refer only to that picture. Arthur then asked Mary what would be on the right of the door into her drawing room, and did she have an owl in the form of a picture or ornament? Andrew said he would be standing next to the owl at 9 p.m. that evening. The owl was a little silver ornament Andrew had given to her and it was on the end of a bookcase opposite to where she sat. She did not see Andrew that evening but felt something else would come of it.

Mary worked as a healer, therapist and teacher. Some weeks later she was talking to a patient who was a very conservative lady, definitely not a spiritualist, who had never met Andrew when he was in this world, but had seen his photographs displayed around Mary's home. She told Mary she had seen the spirit of her son standing next to the owl and looking at them in a very serious way, which was his normal look. Where 9 p.m. fitted in was never quite clear. Often people do not see as deeply into messages as they merit, though I doubt if this would apply to Mary. On another occasion Andrew communicated the following words to Mary: 'You gave me life once, can I live again through you? Let me live again as I want to guide and inspire you.'

After reading this story one could question the evidence given in so far as we tend to expect all the *i*s dotted and the *t*s crossed. In my opinion the best evidence lies in what Arthur does, which is to give the feeling that the communicator is right there in the room at the same time, talking about little personal things which would mean so much to the recipient but not to anyone else. This is where Arthur excels.


Although Arthur's work often brings him into contact with people struggling with deep grief, he is alive to the humour that can sometimes arise at even the darkest of times. He recalls with sadness but also humour the occasion when a young man consulted him whose mother had committed suicide. Naturally, an extremely sensitive and emotionally charged atmosphere pervaded the room. The young man sat on the edge of his chair listening eagerly so as not to miss a word his mother might say. Behind the fireplace in the room, and coming from the adjoining building, there must have been an intercom system to the front door two floors down. At times one could hear part of a conversation when someone was answering the intercom. As Arthur was relaying what his mother had to say, a woman's voice was heard to say: 'Is there anybody there?' The grief-stricken son looked up to the ceiling and said, 'Yes, Mum, it's me.' Arthur did not have the heart to tell him it wasn't her and let it pass. He continued helping the young man and sent him away happy. I think it is fair to say it may have been a coincidence, although it may have been designed and timed to happen at the right time. Who knows? What provides a touch of humour to us now gave reassurance to someone in need at the time.

Which leads to another humorous story. When Arthur was giving a reading to a titled lady who looked just like one's idea of a duchess, the outside of the College of Psychic Studies was being decorated. Being a hot summer's day, the windows were open and one could hear the voices of the Irish workmen on the scaffolding outside. The main communicator for this lady was her husband, who was Irish by birth. As Arthur spoke the words 'Your husband wants to tell you . . .' the Irishman working on the floor above yelled to his workmates downstairs: 'Get your "so and so" backside up here,' only in much more vulgar terms. The lady was shaken to her foundations and Arthur had to explain what was happening. Like all ladies of breeding she quickly regained her composure and said: 'Oh good, he doesn't want me up there yet!'

Arthur's grandmother
Cristobalina Rio Roja

Arthur's parents
Cecilia and Arturo

Arthur Molinary as little boy
aged 7 at confirmation

Arthur Molinary

Arthur's son and his wife, Roland and Ruth

Arthur's grandchildren, Left to right: Hazel, Heather and Emma

Above: Arthur with sister Jeronima and brother-in-law Humberto

Left: Arthur with portrait painted by Clifford Fisher which now hangs in College of Psychic Studies

# 6

## *In Gibraltar and the Princess*

When Arthur met Mrs Peta Pryor for the first time, Arthur described her as having a very happy face, a cheerful personality and a bagful of troubles. She had two husbands in the spirit world but the more important of the two, called Richard, became the main communicator. Arthur felt he was being spoken to by a schoolteacher. Peta quickly confirmed Richard was one. Arthur heard Richard saying, 'See you at the Marina', and immediately got a picture in mind of the only Marina he knew, a restaurant located in La Linea in southern Spain. In fact, Peta and Richard had lived in Gibraltar and had frequented the restaurant quite often. Richard then spoke of a black cat sitting on his grave back in Gibraltar. Peta said it was a dog and not a cat. Richard's favourite dog died soon after him and Peta had a clay model made to put on his grave. Richard, however, repeated the communication insistently: 'There is a black cat sitting on my grave,' and the only answer Peta could give was, 'I think he's lost it, poor dear.' She had quite forgotten this communication when she visited the cemetery again and was amazed to find a real black cat sitting next to the model dog. (Another good instance of a message that seems 'wrong' at the time but which later turns out to be true.) Arthur also gave Peta more evidence from her parents, sister Daphne and a previous husband, nicknamed Butch, whose surname was Bacheler.

Peta was so pleased with her reading that she asked Arthur if he would visit Gibraltar to work and he gladly agreed, being eager to revisit his homeland. Peta met him at the airport and took him to her house in La Linea, which was quite impressive. Here Arthur's humour found another outlet when she showed him where he would sleep. The bed had previously been occupied by the well-known medium Doris Stokes. Arthur joked to Peta: 'I hope you have changed the sheets since.'

Arthur was happy to be back in Gibraltar, a place which held so many memories for him. Peta owned a health store there and advertised Arthur's visit by putting a poster in the shop window stating: 'Gibraltar's own medium who also speaks Spanish.' She also had an enlarged photo of him in the store so her customers would see it as they went in. Needless to say he was heavily booked and in great demand. Whilst in Gibraltar Arthur also broadcast a very successful chat show on the local radio station and began to realise how much the people were proud of their 'Gibraltar-born medium'.

One of his readings he gave was to a Mrs Posso in her home. When she opened the door she was dressed in black from head to toe, as is the wont of a lot of the older generation in that part of the world. As she led him into her sitting room, Arthur observed a picture of a young man hanging on a wall. Around it were fairy lights and on a small shelf nearby were flowers and candles. Arthur knew it signified the young man was dead. The first communicator, however, was her late husband. Arthur saw him carrying newspapers, sweets and tobacco, and walking towards a kiosk near El Martello ('The Hammer'). Mrs Posso said her husband had worked there. He continued to give very personal messages for his wife through Arthur, all of which she accepted.

Next he saw two young men in their late teens, and as one stepped forwards he told Mrs Posso it was her son. To which she replied, 'No, my son is alive.' The young man, as Arthur saw him, stepped further forward and appeared to have a bundle under his right arm, which he then placed in front of Arthur and unwrapped it. The contents was a dead chicken next to which the son placed a few coins. On relating this to Mrs Posso she just sat in her armchair shaking her head. She insisted the information was very interesting but that her son was still alive. After the reading Arthur talked to her for a while. Then, as he got up to leave, she noticed he was staring at the picture of her son and the fairy lights. Noticing she had become a little sad, Arthur said: 'Your son was a nice-looking young man.' Mrs Posso went on to tell him that, eight years before, her son and his best friend had gone on a day trip to Morocco and that before they had left she had given him a thousand-peseta note to bring her back a chicken and any change. The boys never came back home. They had been reported missing but Mrs Posso was sure one day they would both come back home.

The next day Mrs Posso telephoned Peta Pryor and asked for another reading with Arthur. She'd had time to think and wanted to communicate with her husband again. Unfortunately Arthur was too busy but in any case could not bear to repeat what he knew to be true but which she refused to accept: her son was dead. In a strange way maybe it was best that she continued to hope for her son's return. After all, one day there would be a happy reunion, though not in this world.

One day while waiting for Peta, Arthur sat and turned over in his mind a question she had asked him: whether to sell the store or hang on to it. Suddenly he became aware of a man in his early twenties who appeared to be tidying the shelves, which were not, as Arthur was currently seeing it, stacked with vitamin bottles but with clothes. The man looked at him and said: 'Tell Peta not to sell up as she needs something to do with her days and the store will keep doing well.' Arthur felt the man had drowned in a most horrific way.

When Peta returned Arthur told her what he had experienced. She told him the store had originally belonged to two brothers who had sold clothes. She bought the store from one of them. She went on to relate how the brothers had taken a day off to go fishing and that whilst out at sea in the Straits of Gibraltar one of them had dived in for a swim. He developed cramps and called for his brother to help, who promptly dived in and managed to get him back to the boat. Totally exhausted, the brother managed to push him back on board the vessel but was himself pulled under by the treacherous currents and drowned. After the tragedy the remaining brother did not want anything more to do with the shop and sold it to Peta.

When walking with Peta in the Alameda Gardens, they sat down to rest on one of the benches. Almost immediately Arthur became aware of a man who had hanged himself somewhere nearby, and told Peta what he was experiencing. Peta pointed out a big tree where a man had indeed hanged himself. Apparently lots of mediums had sensed this, and the suicide had been the first communicator at one of Doris Stokes' big public demonstrations. Perhaps he needed to do a 'star turn', as it seems he made regular comebacks!


Arthur deals with all kinds of personalities but sees everyone on the same level. In his words, 'lives are as different as they are the same. Pain is pain and fire in any language is just as hot.'

On New Year's Eve in 1988 he was invited to a party by some good friends in their home just opposite Kensington Palace. Not being a party person but having agreed to go, he wondered how he could arrange to arrive late and leave early. It was 11.30 p.m. when he reluctantly arrived to find the party was in full swing. After being greeted by his host and hostess he was given a drink and told to mingle. He found a quiet corner where he could sit and just watch the partygoers. Suddenly out of the corner of his eye he saw a lady making her way towards him. By her unsteady gait it was obvious she had been drinking quite a lot. She sat right down beside him and said, 'You may call me Your Royal Highness.'

With typical sardonic humour Arthur replied: 'Sorry, madam, but I have problems with long words, so may I call you Toots?' She found this very amusing and as she laughed she placed her arm over Arthur's and gave him a big smile. Taking another sip from her drink she began to sing something from *Porgy and Bess* with the opening words 'Fish gotta swim, birds gotta fly', except she had the fish flying and the birds swimming. Stopping herself, she added, 'Why is this room on a hill?'

Although she was somewhat intoxicated she was still in control of her senses. After a New Year's kiss and greetings she talked to Arthur and poured out her troubles. He knew she was a lady from the highest family in the land, who had everything and the world at her feet, but he also sensed her heart was aching and empty. Princess Margaret had found someone to talk to who understood and perhaps it was her need to do that directed her to Arthur, even though she was tipsy. He has that special quality which radiates to anyone of any rank in need.

When Arthur travels to work it is by a number 49 bus which passes the main entrance to Kensington Palace. The bus travels along Kensington Road and as it does so it is possible for passengers on the top deck to see large areas of Kensington Gardens. Until August 1997 it was just a park but the following month it became a place of national pilgrimage

61

where people brought their flowers and gifts to show their love and respect for Princess Diana, who, as we all know, had been killed in a tragic accident. It transformed the scene into a kaleidoscope of colours and Arthur could sense the 'ordinary' person who had helped create the tidal wave of energy. The Princess was an 'ingredient' in the making of this energy from which any sensitive individual can benefit as they pass by. Every morning Arthur passes her front door and mentally says 'Good morning, Diana' and asks her whether, if she gets a free moment, she would like to help him with his work.

Many may think this to be nonsense, but in fact the whole universe is buzzing with energies and vibrations that can be used for good or bad. If we take the right attitude and approach, it is possible to become more aware of these energies, and get the best out of life. Arthur approaches this with what may appear to be a simple, even childlike, attitude. Arthur not only listens but observes and searches for his inner feelings. In my opinion, in order to become a good medium or psychic one needs to be aware of both the 'inner' and the 'outer' forces and learn how to make them work together. Arthur often mentions how his grandmother often told him that whenever she had a problem or sadness of heart, she would tell the little sparrow to fly away and tell other birds. This he took to mean that he should let his feelings go out and into the atmosphere and then by listening to the atmosphere it would talk back to him.

Arthur is very sensitive to the grief and despair of those who lose their loved ones, especially children and those taken off by unhappy circumstances. He feels all he can offer is a few words of comfort along with the evidence to reassure them that all is not lost.

Mr and Mrs Morrison, who lived in Ealing Common,

wrote to Arthur asking him to visit their daughter's apartment in order to solve a mystery, if possible. Once there and tuning in, he felt the only communicator was a young woman, good at business and with a clear thinking mind. He could not sense any illness with her but felt a sharp pain inside his head, which was what she must have experienced just before she died. Eventually her mother asked outright how her daughter had died. Immediately he had a mental vision. Frances was taking him along to the front door of the apartment. He heard the doorbell ring and as she opened the door he saw a crouching woman who appeared to be holding a small crossbow. Immediately an arrow left the weapon and entered Frances's head. In reality, because of the firing angle the arrow had entered through Frances's throat and passed straight into her brain.

Despite the speed with which it happened, Frances did recognise her assailant, calling out 'No, Maureen!' When asked if she knew who Maureen was, Mrs Morrison glanced across at her husband, as if they had suspected this all along. She then said Frances's boyfriend, Mark, had had an ex-girlfriend called Maureen who was very jealous of him. She had vowed she would kill anyone who took her place.

Frances told Arthur the murder weapon was hanging on a wall with lots of other weapons in Putney. This unfortunately was rather vague information and Frances failed to pass on any more detail. Which means that Maureen is still free to roam; the police could not find any connections or trace the killer. It all remains a mystery but at least the Morrisons had confirmation of the identity of their daughter's killer but admitted that justice, sadly, could not be done. How does one comfort the aching heart of a parent when their child dies? A mother shares her body with an unborn child for nine months and after its birth both parents give love and caring to their offspring. When a son or daughter dies for whatever reason, the rest of the family grieves for ever.

# 7

## *Wormwood Scrubs*

Arthur has done a lot of work in helping criminals. Having read of mediums visiting prison before, Arthur was very interested when the then President of the College of Psychic Studies received a letter from Wormwood Scrubs prison. It was from a man serving 'life' for his crimes, asking if one of the College mediums would go along to give him a reading. Lifers are not normally allowed such privileges, so it was necessary to obtain permission from the Home Office. Since Arthur lived close to the prison and was believed to be the best one to handle such a delicate situation, he was chosen to be the first medium ever to give a reading to a lifer. He was happy and willing to do so: it was, for him, another challenge.

Arthur received a visitor's permit and went along to do the reading, not knowing quite what to expect. Having never before been inside a prison, he found this one to be as depressing on the inside as it was on the outside. The guards were stern but friendly and after putting him through the usual security checks he was told to report to the guard at the prisoner's canteen. Here he was directed to table number 52 and told to wait for Mr John Copley. Eventually the lifer appeared: a man of small stature with a pleasant face, quite jolly and with a heavy northern accent. Ten minutes later, a guard appeared and took them to a very tiny room containing only two chairs. There was a glass door through which the guard could sit and watch. Arthur was so stressed out that he cannot remember much of this first reading at all.

When John next corresponded with Arthur he told him he was being moved down to Lewes in Sussex. They continued to keep in touch by letter until Arthur was able to make the journey to Lewes, which turned out to be a brighter prison than the one before. It was the same routine as last time except they sat in the visitors' café. After a few minutes a man came and sat at their table. John introduced him and the man told Arthur he was another lifer, John's next-door cellmate. Obviously John had told him who Arthur was and what he did because the conversation kept turning back to mediumship. The man, as Arthur only realised later, turned out to be the notorious Reggie Kray, and during the brief, seven-minute reading that followed Arthur was able to pass on information from Reggie's mother – information, Reggie told him, that only she could have known; not even his brother knew about these things.

John once told Arthur of something that had happened to him when he was fourteen. He had just started work as an underground pony driver in Kirkley Colliery in Yorkshire. During a twenty-minute break one day, he felt as though his pony, Paul, was communicating with him using some kind of telepathy. He had a vision in which he saw men running along the narrow roadway away from the coalface. He felt within himself the vibrations of a thunderous roar which he described as like 'Armageddon' and saw steam swirling around the men. A dark-grey depression surrounded the immediate area and then the scene faded. The vision recurred four or five times during John's working day. Later, when he took Paul to the meadow and let him loose, it was as though the pony's eyes were telling him that what he had seen in his vision was about to happen.

The following day John felt a terrible uneasiness and at 8 a.m. he spoke to William, the man in charge, and told him about his vision. William responded with laughter and said, 'The roof's as safe as houses; you've been dreaming, lad!' At 9 a.m. John sat down to his snack, his pony beside him waiting for titbits. Almost immediately the pony started to stamp his hooves and snort. John knew something was wrong and walked fifty yards or so towards the coalface. Paul became very agitated and, as he followed John, he nudged his bare back with his wet muzzle a couple of times. As they got to within twenty yards of the coalface Paul snorted and ran fast back towards their resting place. As John reached a spot about five or six yards from the coalface he could hear the snapping and crackling of wooden props that supported the face and roof. One of his colleagues was shouting, 'Get out, it's coming in!'

John was the first to run back along the narrow roadway with all the men following fast on his heels. With a thunderous roar, three whole stalls caved in. Hot steaming air pushed the men several feet along the roadway which they could hear crashing behind them, just seconds away. When they reached the clearing, the tunnel had stopped collapsing just five feet from the men. Most of them were stripped to the waist because of the heat in the roadways and the hot blast of air had scorched their skins. There weren't any fatalities or injuries but just ten seconds had separated them from being entombed for ever.

After Lewes, John was moved again, this time to a prison in Huntingdon, Cambridgeshire. Because of Arthur's increasingly busy and demanding life, the pen-friendship started to fade and finally stopped. He knew John had a very bad chest and was hard of hearing through working down coal mines and the after-effects of an explosion. He learnt later that John Copley had died aged seventy-one whilst still in custody at Kingston.

\* \* \*

Arthur has also worked on the other side of the law – giving readings to policemen, barristers, judges and solicitors. When Dorit Chomer LLB (Hons), a lawyer, visited the College for the first time, she was in for a very big surprise. At home she had watched Shirley MacLaine on television and picked up the term 'trance channeller', so she felt she had to see one. When she eventually discovered the College it filled her with doubts. From the outside it seemed almost too ordinary but she decided to check it out.

Her first surprise came when she asked to see a trance channeller and was told by what she described as an ordinary-looking receptionist sitting behind an ordinary-looking desk that they didn't have any of those but did have mediums. She decided she would try one and asked to see someone who could contact her father, who had died ten years earlier. The receptionist pointed to someone standing behind Dorit and she turned to see an ordinary-looking man, drinking an ordinary cup of tea, wearing a shirt and tie with a V-neck pullover. He could have been mistaken for a businessman. She really expected to see someone with a white face and long hair, dripping with jewellery and clutching a crystal ball. Instead of that she got Arthur Molinary!

Arthur agreed to help her but she was still suspicious. How would she know Arthur was talking to her father at all? Arthur replied: 'We'll ask him to prove it!' Being a lawyer she liked that and asked how soon she could see him. 'Now,' interrupted the receptionist. 'There's been a last-minute cancellation.' This further aroused Dorit's suspicions as she thought he would be, as she put it, 'not much cop'. She had seen him as someone standing around drinking tea and waiting for some poor lost soul like her to come through the door. However, she paid her fee and walked up the stairs to Room No. 3 where Arthur was now waiting. In her own words she said:

Little did I know that when I walked into that room, I would walk out a different person. That this man would play a large part in my life as well as my mother's, sister's, cousins' and friends' lives for the next ten years and hopefully more.

Her first words to Arthur were, 'So, mister, let's have some proof!' He began by telling her some things about her aura but this did not interest her. However, having paid her money, she thought she wouldn't get a refund, so she decided to 'shut up and sit up'. She later saw how her behaviour must have been considered rude but by then had realised that Arthur must have seen the deep pain she was hiding.

The next forty-five minutes had Dorit sitting on the edge of her seat in a mixture of disbelief, shock and amazement. She instantly felt she was prepared to sit on Arthur's doorstep and see him every day. To Arthur it was all in a day's work but to Dorit it had changed her life.

His first impression was of a man coming towards them, breathing heavily. He punched Arthur's cheek and slapped him on the back as a form of greeting. Dorit felt this could be her father: he was an Egyptian and greeted everyone that way. He told her he was sorry he wasn't able to say goodbye to the three of them. Her father died in Turkey whilst she, her mother and sister were all in different places. Dorit felt Arthur should be able to tell her something she didn't know. As if he had read her mind he said, 'Where would I find a picture or statue of a dolphin?' She thought it a stupid question: what did that have to do with her dad? She asked if it could be in a book? Arthur said, 'No, that's not what I am looking for. Can you please check that out with your mother?' Again Dorit considered this to be a waste of time; her father had been a big businessman who travelled around the world and would have had no time for animals and the like. Later she checked with her mother who told her dolphins were 'Dad's lucky charm' and that he always carried some dolphin trinket in his pocket to bring him luck in business.

Later in the reading, Arthur asked her why she would want to name a child Rachael? At this time Dorit was in her second week of pregnancy and had decided, if it was a girl, she would call her after her grandmother – Rachael. Arthur's words made her feel sure she was carrying a baby girl and in the following April she did give birth to her daughter Rachael. Next an aunt communicated and said she was pulling her son's carpet all the time to straighten it up. Dorit said her cousin David had a rug on his carpet which was always buckling. Arthur also said her aunt had an ice cube in her mouth when she died. This was true as, owing to illness, she couldn't drink fluids, which Dorit only found out later. He also said Dorit's sister had a kidney problem and should get it checked out. Later Dorit heard her sister was already in hospital with that problem.

Dorit considered she was a 'hard nut to crack', but Arthur continued to 'hit her' with more amazing things. Some items he called 'stupid trivia', things that at the time meant nothing but would work out later. He told her a cousin would be going to a wedding where he'd meet a girl he would want to marry. A few months later her cousin Hain did in fact receive and accept an invitation to a wedding and with exactly those happy consequences.

Dorit was so amazed by the reading that she wanted to book with Arthur again for the following day, but was informed that he was so much in demand that she could only get an appointment every six months or so. She told the receptionist 'He's an amazing guy', to which that lady replied, 'We know!' So she had to be content with returning home with the tape recording of her reading, which she subsequently listened to so many times that it nearly wore out. During the next ten years she saw Arthur once or twice a year. One year she got three readings by giving a fake name. Such was her absolute belief he had contacted her dad and others 'over there', that she would have done anything to keep up that contact through Arthur. Unsurprisingly, she also recommended Arthur to her friends and family.

Dorit's sister Shula was told by her father in a reading that a member of her family would come and ask her to buy some land in a part of Israel that was under development but which at the time seemed like a bad investment. This was followed by asking Shula if she knew anyone from Mexico, which at the time she didn't. A few months later a cousin from Mexico unexpectedly turned up and asked Shula to join her in a property speculation deal in a remote part of Israel. The land was worth £35,000, which at the time was a lot of money, and Shula's husband refused to let her part with the cash. Today the land is worth £175,000. Arthur told Dorit's mother that someone called Sally would look after her as something was wrong with her hip. At the time her mother's hip was fine but two years later she fell and broke it. When she was sent home from hospital she needed a nurse to look after her. After a long search a neighbour who had the requisite qualifications was found and, not surprisingly, her name was Sally.

Arthur also told Dorit that William from the BBC would contact her and she would be on the television and radio as well as in the newspapers. Out of the blue some time later a certain William called and asked her to go on breakfast television. Her appearance on the programme provoked an avalanche of calls from the media. She was interviewed on radio and a newspaper did a feature on her company. For a few months she became famous in the educational world and the publicity did wonders for her business. She had forgotten all about Arthur's prediction until she replayed a tape recording with the communication.

Dorit's tapes of readings always gave her great comfort and reassurance, and listening, especially in times of need, always brought her close to her dad. On one occasion Arthur told Dorit her dad was concerned about the smell of urine around her mother and thought it could be an infection. Dorit telephoned her sister in Israel to ask if Mum was well, only to be told she wasn't, owing to a urine infection. When Dorit told her that she already knew, her sister asked how she possibly could when she lived five thousand miles away. 'Arthur told me!' was Dorit's reply.

Arthur once told Dorit about a vision he had where she was sitting in her bedroom and getting a great feeling of luck. He could not explain why but felt that, if she in some way changed her bed, her whole outlook on life and living would change, she would feel a lot better and things would start to get brighter. She would feel right, in a way she had never felt before. Dorit, however, did not want to buy a new bed, even though Arthur reminded her he hadn't exactly said she should. Some time later, when Dorit attended a 'Mind, Body and Spirit' exhibition, she found herself at a stand where they sold therapeutic magnets to heal back pain. At first she thought it was just a new fad until the saleswoman told her about a new bed system involving magnets that was supposed to help back sufferers. Dorit was no ordinary back sufferer: she had been nearly paralysed after a parachute accident fifteen years earlier. By her own admission, she was a 'professional' back sufferer and had tried all the back 'toys' God had ever invented, and some he hadn't. The lady lent her a magnetic duvet for a week's trial. It worked wonders, for when she awoke the next day she was pain free. So she bought the unit and one each for her mother and her three children, who still use them. After all the years of suffering Dorit found this one duvet had changed her life because now she could walk around painlessly and with a straight back. She had forgotten once again what her dad had said through Arthur until she listened to the tape again, and it all fell into place. When she next saw Arthur, she told him: 'Damn, you're good!'

*  *  *

Everything in Arthur's daily life is set to music and song. One day he awoke to hear in his mind the song 'Moody River', as sung by Pat Boone. It was as though the record had stuck at one point and kept repeating over and over: 'Moody river more deadly than the vainest night, moody river your muddy waters took my baby's life'. This persisted until the following day when he heard the news of an accident on the River Thames where a boat called the *Marchioness* had crashed into another vessel and sunk. It happened at night when there were many young people on board, several of whom were drowned. Arthur was subsequently consulted by a lady who received evidential communication, through his mediumship, from her beautiful young daughter who was tragically drowned on that ill-fated vessel.

On another occasion Arthur awoke 'hearing' the words of a song especially written for the death of President John F. Kennedy. The song says 'Shot down in a Texas town in the summer of his years'. In his head all he could hear repeatedly was 'in the summer of his years'. Next day he heard the news of the death of Princess Diana. Many experience these kind of messages but aren't able to take them further. In receiving psychic communication of any kind, it has to come through the mind, and so much depends on how the individual mind works and interprets what comes through.

# 8

## *Enduring Love*

When Phillipa saw Arthur for a reading she told him that she didn't believe in an afterlife, but had heard from friends that he comforted people. After his customary aura reading, Arthur told her she had a husband in the spirit world. He could not ascertain the cause of her husband's passing but felt he had died quickly. He then passed on messages that were more personal but confirmed how much they loved each other. He asked Phillipa why he was seeing what is known as a 'desert rose' – a rose-like pattern caused by residual moisture that sometimes forms in the desert. She replied that she and her husband had spent their honeymoon in the Sahara and that his name for her was Desert Rose!

Phillipa then asked Arthur whether there was anyone else there. Immediately he felt there was a young man who must have been their son, who, unlike her husband, must have suffered, to which she agreed. Arthur had the feeling of spiders crawling over him, which usually denotes the communicator died of cancer, which proved to be right. Phillipa said she felt guilty because she, too, had had cancer but it had been caught early and cured. Despite this communication, Phillipa was still having doubts about the existence of an afterlife. Arthur offered comfort, but could he prove survival? As if to reply to these doubts, her son said: 'How would you feel if you found a white feather in the bedroom?' She replied she had an allergy to birds and her bedroom was double-glazed so that nothing could get in. Her son still insisted she would find the feather.

On her second visit to Arthur, Phillipa immediately told him she still did not believe in an afterlife, although she admitted that, on returning home from the last reading, she had found a white feather on her bedroom carpet. Her real reason for seeing Arthur again was the fact she was suspicious that Arthur must have known where she lived and had somehow already collated details about her life. Naturally he assured her otherwise and went on to give her more evidence. Nonetheless, she left in much the same frame of mind. On her third visit she said she still didn't believe but found comfort in listening to what Arthur had to say. This time Arthur told her he felt as if she was surrounded by pigs, to which she replied she collected pig ornaments. Arthur then added: 'Although you don't believe any of this, your son says that amongst all your pigs you have a monkey.' Her reply was that she had found a key ring with a monkey on it which she kept with her collection of pigs. Whether she left with any belief in an afterlife is uncertain but presumably she had found more comfort, so time and effort had not been wasted.


We all encounter 'cranks' in this work. Arthur certainly does. He told me about one, a very handsome, smartly dressed young man who came for a reading. After ten minutes he said to Arthur, 'Don't you know who I am?' At first Arthur thought he was in show business in some way, but decided to he honest and say he didn't know. The sitter told him, 'I am Jesus Christ.' This caught Arthur off guard. Not knowing quite what to do, he got up and walked across to the man, shook his hand and said, 'Pleased to meet you, Lord.' He then returned to his seat and continued with the reading.

One often needs a sense of humour to deal with such situations that might otherwise have developed badly.

I recall an occasion when I was lecturing in a crowded hall when a young man, who also claimed to be Jesus, came up to the stage and tried to strangle me because he was unhappy with the answers I gave to his questions. Fortunately he was restrained. I doubt if it was the same man who consulted Arthur but, alas, the world is full of would-be Jesus Christs.

Many people believe in reincarnation and believe they have had past lives. It is a very debatable subject which I have investigated and think there is a possibility but not enough real evidence to support it. Arthur has no interest in past lives because he thinks he has enough problems to deal with in this one. He recalls a reading when he felt the lady sitter radiated 'Hollywood glamour' as she entered the room. The reading went well until near the end when the lady appeared to be fidgeting. When asked what was the matter she replied, 'Well, you haven't told me about my past life.' Arthur asked whether she new she had lived previously. She became angry and said, 'Yes, I was Cleopatra.' He suddenly felt his hackles rising and said, 'Excuse me, madam, but I'm a little confused. One of our receptionists also claims to have been Cleopatra.' As she departed in a huff, Arthur told her she was the ninth Cleopatra he had met so far.

Arthur has his own personal beliefs but tries to keep them private. He hates people trying to push their beliefs down his throat and tries to avoid doing it to others himself. Anyone can believe in whatever gives them the required strength to cope with their lives. If anyone uses another's energies to help them, then so be it, as long as it's done without a fuss. He quotes his grandmother who used to say, 'When I come over to your house I will listen to your troubles and beliefs, and when you come to me you listen to mine.' Wise words indeed.

He tends to get annoyed with talk about 'chakras', which is an Eastern word referring to the 'nerve centres' of the body and which had become very fashionable to speak about. In his early days at the College he recalls a lady arriving late for her appointment in a very agitated state. She sat down and then asked Arthur, 'Would you like me to open up my chakras?' To which he replied, 'No, madam, you sit there and keep everything closed as I'm doing all the work today.' This is typical of a man who tends to be a little too forthright and 'John Blunt' but it never stops him giving of his best, no matter who and what the situation.

Elaine first saw Arthur at a time when she was exhausted by the demands of a busy and stressful job. She had a widowed father living on his own, ninety miles away and confined to a wheelchair, who received some assistance from carers. She also had a difficult situation with her son, who also had health problems. Arthur immediately said her mother, who was in the other world, although not good at displaying warmth and emotion when here, was now giving support and help. She told her she was particularly keen to help her granddaughter who, in pursuing a career on the musical stage, was fulfilling her own frustrated ambitions. Elaine's mother compared her granddaughter to Georgia Brown, a famous singing star, saying she had presence, voice and charisma but did not know it. She would have to deal with the 'shark-infested' waters of show business but would come to be sought after. The next year would be full of work in a musical comedy filled with American energy. Elaine's daughter was subsequently offered a year's contract to tour in a production of the Cole Porter musical *Kiss Me Kate*.

Elaine's son was suffering from Crohn's disease, and at the time was entering a particularly bad episode. Arthur identified his problem and current situation. She was surprised, when, after all her responsibilities had caused her to wonder how much longer she could keep up with her job *and* caring, Arthur said she would be working month after month with a committee. He saw blueprints and plans of a building and she would be involved in a project to build a concert hall. He said she was not going to retire in the immediate future but would be given more responsibility. He mentioned an Andy or Andreas, which at the time meant nothing. A year later she was working on just such a project with a new trustee named Andreas, called Andy for short.

Arthur also told Elaine that the period from the 17th of August to September would be important to her, and it transpired her father became increasingly ill then and died in September. Later he also told her about when her father died and gave a good description of him and her mother, including events in their younger days of which Elaine had only just become aware. Things Arthur could not possibly have known. Elaine received a lot of personal and private information which gave her great insight into, and confidence about, her son and daughter. She felt reassured about the future.

# 9

## Anne Shelton and 'Absent Friends'

In 1960 Arthur first saw and heard a wonderful lady singing in the well-known television show *Sunday Night at the London Palladium*. The warmth of her personality and remarkable voice made him anxious to hear more. At this time he was working as a book-restoration specialist, which is a lonely job. He frequently listened to the radio whilst working and was overjoyed to hear a programme called *Worker's Playtime* on which Anne Shelton often sang.

Not only did she sing for the workers but as a teenager had also entertained the RAF during the Second World War, becoming known as a Forces Sweetheart. She was universally loved for her unique voice and singing style which took her to the heights of stardom on both sides of the Atlantic. Those who were lucky enough to see Anne could not fail to love her, not only for her singing, but her impressive presence. Beautiful, glamorous, smartly dressed and elegant, she was a star to her fingertips. She was a favourite of Arthur's mother and was very high on Arthur's list, too. He has many favourites among her songs but the one that is always in the forefront of his mind as being most applicable to his career as a medium is called 'Absent Friends'. It contains the line 'Raise up your glass and drink to absent friends'.

After he left his job and became a professional medium, imagine Arthur's surprise and delight when Anne Shelton, OBE, came into his room for a reading. He remembers her as a very dignified lady who insisted on calling him Mr Molinary and not Arthur. Larger than life, impeccably groomed and dressed, she sat in an armchair and made her overwhelming presence felt. However, she was sad and somewhat nervous. She had never been to a medium before and was naturally apprehensive, making it quite clear she wanted words of reassurance about members of her family who had passed on. It was important for her to know they were free from pain and at peace.

She was a very religious lady with her own beliefs but respecting those of others. She had always been a big lady but that day she appeared to have lost weight due to grieving for her husband and sister Jo, who had also been a performer. In giving evidence of their survival, Arthur was reminded of the time he saw Jo make her own singing debut on *Sunday Night at the London Palladium*. Jo was Anne's closest friend in a very close-knit family.

In the first reading Arthur heard Latin music, then in his mind saw a room where there were straight, hard-backed chairs around a table on which lay a gold record. Anne replied that Latin music was her favourite and that the table and chairs were her own. The gold record (disc) was an award given by the United Nations for recording the song 'Greensleeves' with Yul Brynner for the Save the Children charity. During the same reading Jo came through to Anne and said she was dancing with David; she had no pain and was laughing again. She told Anne that the nail varnish she was wearing was 'not hers'. In actual fact they both wore the same colour, but since her death Anne had been using Jo's bottle of nail varnish, and was wearing it that very day. Jo told Anne she must carry on working and she would always be with her – by the side of the stage as before. Jo told Anne she must be strong for Eileen, her remaining older sister and Kelly Richards, her niece.

Anne died in July 1994, which was the same month as her sister. She always felt this would be so.

Later Arthur also did readings for Kelly. In one reading
with Arthur, Kelly's mother and two aunts communicated.
He described them as being three little fairies from Sleeping
Beauty, always together and always there for her. Kelly's
father also communicated, saying he would always be around
for her. Arthur then told her: 'He would like to sweep her
like one would a chimney as she was full of other people's
problems and not on top of herself at the time.' This was
true as Kelly was emotionally drained and coming to terms
with the loss of her Aunt Patty (Patricia was Anne Shelton's
real name), with whom she had been very close. In fact she
sometimes used to think she had three mothers! Arthur went
on to say Aunt Patty was communicating and was very
grateful and untouched by life's grime, that her 'baby' (a
name she often called Kelly by) is loved with great tenderness
and she never wants her to be upset. Then he described a
room Anne was showing him, which she called 'her room'
and of which she was proud. She mentioned a gold disc
hanging on a wall and told him about all the memorabilia
the room contained. There were many treasures from her
past, one of which was the gold disc she had received from
the United Nations. The amazing thing about this is that, at
the time of the reading, the room was part of a new extension
still being built in Kelly's home and was to house a collection
of Anne's treasures as a way of honouring her achievements.

Arthur told Kelly the shoes she was wearing were not
hers, to which she replied that they were a pair she had
bought for her aunt; they were a little tight so she had asked
Kelly to break them in for her. Before she had had a chance
to do so, Anne had sadly passed on. Arthur described Anne
as being a family lady who enjoyed her privacy. She was
now injecting strength into Kelly whose own mother was
dying. He said Kelly's aunts were waiting for her mum. The
day before Kelly's mum passed away, she held out her hand
towards the doorway of her room and said 'Pat' and 'Jo';

Kelly felt her aunts had come to take her mother to the spirit world. Arthur said there would be a 6 or 10 in connection with her mother's passing, maybe June or October as they were the sixth and tenth month; he couldn't be more specific. Her mother died on 5th September 1996 at 6.10 p.m.

Arthur told Kelly her Aunt Patty was a bright, light-hearted spirit with a song in her heart and wanted her to be likewise; that during the summer months she would be sitting with her in a place in her garden, sheltered from the sun, with two seats under an arbour. Kelly said she had already felt Anne there very strongly. Anne said she could never imagine Kelly's home without music, which was true. Kelly and her partner, Di, have varying tastes and there is always music playing. She also said the last two years for Kelly had been very hard but she should 'lay down her arms and surrender'. Words from a song that Anne made famous. Kelly told Arthur it had been a number-one hit in 1956. During the communication Arthur said he felt pains in his chest. Anne had suffered a major heart attack. He asked Kelly if she could understand why he felt he was holding a paper tissue in his hand at the time of the pains. To this she replied that Anne had died sitting up in bed holding a paper tissue. He told Kelly her aunts were her guardians as well as her mother.

Anne appeared to be making 'a sign of the cross' on Arthur's back. He asked if it had any relevance. Kelly explained how it had become a lucky ritual that Anne and her sister Jo (and after Jo's passing, Kelly herself) did before Anne went on stage. Anne told Kelly she had felt no sadness in passing and had gone out like a light. She'd had enough since losing most of her loved ones and wished to be reunited with them.

The evidence that Anne gave to Kelly through Arthur's mediumship has been enough to show this great lady of song has survived and is happily settled in her new life. It would be easy to imagine her giving concerts to the many thousands of 'spirit fans' who are with her. Even today many of my circle still remember her and listen to her recordings. Communication is a two-way thing and if thoughts can reach out, and I believe they do, then Anne will know how much she is still loved and appreciated for all the pleasure she gave the world.


Often when people enter Arthur's room for a reading he gets very strong feelings as soon as they walk in, even before they take their coat off and sit down. When Fatima came to see him, the moment she walked in he had a picture in his mind's eye of little chocolate Easter bunnies with ribbons and a little bell around their necks. After she had settled down, the first communicator was her father who had passed just three weeks earlier. In giving a good description of him and how he died, Arthur told her he came with two young men, one of whom was in his twenties and the other in his teens. Fatima told him they were her sons. Arthur asked her what the older son had to do with aeroplanes and she said he was a flying instructor. He then told her he felt he was going through the clouds and crashing to the ground, to which she said that nobody knows why the plane crashed. Fatima went on to explain how all her family had gone away for Easter, but her eldest son was taking his younger brother home for dinner. The younger boy had wanted to go for a plane ride with his big brother, who, to give his sibling a treat, agreed. The tragedy occurred when the plane 'just fell out of the sky!' Arthur correctly told his sitter there was a two-hour gap between her speaking to her sons and their death. There was no apparent reason for the crash but the boys did not suffer; they had died instantly. The boys communicated a wealth of detail to their mother including the fact he saw lots of toiletries in the bathroom and various things in other places that all appeared to be neat and tidy.

This she confirmed and said that everything was just as they left it. The boys also gave lots of accurate information concerning their two sisters still in this world.

Fatima's father then took over and Arthur said he made him feel as though they were sitting in some kind of palace, to which Fatima replied that her mother lives in a palace. Father said there were a lot of problems due to the fact the mother had a new husband. Fatima explained there were complications between her mother and her second husband and the family. Arthur said he felt the problems between her mother and her youngest daughter arose because they were so similar, whereupon Fatima agreed and said she could not communicate with either of them. After giving the name of the palace and the fact that her mother owned vineyards in Portugal, father talked about problems between Fatima's eldest and youngest brothers that would occur when their mother died. She explained the youngest brother still lived with his mother and often caused scenes over his future inheritance. Then Fatima's flying-instructor son mentioned she had a new boyfriend called Joseph and had miscarried a child by him, which she confirmed. She asked if she would have more children; sadly, the answer was 'no'. Arthur passed on a lot more personal evidence and then asked her where she was flying to on the 17th of June? When she replied, Portugal, both her sons said they would be flying with her to keep her safe.

Arthur concluded by saying that people in the other world usually bring roses but her sons were bringing daises and there had to be a special reason for it. She explained that she was making clay vases and using a daisy pattern to decorate them. Fatima is a doctor and psychologist and not easily taken in, but she received a lot of evidence from the reading which brought her comfort and satisfaction.

\* \* \*

When Richard walked into his room, Arthur asked him if he had been on a beach, because he felt he wanted to shake the sand out of his overalls. He explained to Richard that to him it usually meant that a sitter would be planning to go abroad, as if he or she were shaking out English sand. Immediately Richard's father began to communicate and gave relevant details to his son. Arthur then asked if Richard was having treatment in hospital as he could see a lot of hospital activity around him. To which the reply was no, but that he was the chief chef at a famous London hospital.

Then Arthur sensed Richard's brother, who had died as a young man in his twenties. He had a good sense of humour because he said to Richard: 'You need an appointment to have intimacy with your partner!' The reply was 'True, we rarely have sex together.' On returning to the subject of shaking sand out of overalls, Arthur asked him what link he had with Brazil and why did he and his partner need £30,000 each? Richard told him the reason was because they had been offered a piece of land in Brazil costing £60,000. Then his father symbolically placed a piece of red beef on the table, meaning that Richard's immune system needed building up. Richard explained he was HIV positive and that his dad was correct. The latter imparted a lot more personal information which pleased and helped Richard greatly. He was particularly pleased when Arthur said he would own land in Brazil and it would be near to the ocean. It transpired the land offered to them was indeed quite close to the ocean.

When Hugh Earl saw Arthur he had already received a lot of evidence from a medium called Silvia Popoli. At first he thought Spiritualism and the like was a lot of nonsense. He had a central-heating business and was asked to work on the system at the Spiritualist Association of Great Britain. Apparently an old friend of his who worked there as a healer had told the President Hugh should be given the contract. After a time he realised there might be something in all this psychic 'nonsense' by which he found himself surrounded.

He had lost his six-year-old son to leukaemia and was devastated and suicidal. He was introduced to Silvia Popoli, a well-known and respected medium, who gave him a reading. She told Hugh she could see a young boy named Marc who had ginger hair and was holding up a red football. Hugh could accept this as a description of his son; he had given him a red football for his birthday. Silvia and Hugh got together and felt they were soulmates. She passed on five years later, which led him to see Arthur.

At the first reading Arthur described Silvia in great detail and gave her name. She said, through Arthur, that Hugh had paintings in his bathroom, described his bedroom and his weightlifting trophy with laurel leaves on it. Silvia was saying 'hello' and not 'hi', a greeting she considered to be American and not English. She said he had a baby grand piano and a mirror on the left as he entered his flat. He acknowledged all this to be true. Arthur also described Hugh's mother and father in great detail and mentioned a child lost before he was born.

Despite Hugh's unhappiness and desire to join Silvia, she told him he had a long way to go yet in the earthly world. That he would meet another lady, which he refused to believe until it happened four years later. Silvia also said he had three pairs of brown trousers, links with South Africa, and he had just bought a pair of scissors. All true. Arthur's help, Hugh said, had enriched his life. The world needed more mediums like him.

# 10

## *Psychic Arts at the College of Psychic Studies*

Arthur introduced tarot and palmistry to the College of Psychic Studies and subsequently gave courses on tarot and Spanish sand readings as well as psychic development classes. He proved to be a fine teacher. There were always long waiting lists for his classes just as there are for his personal readings. To some people's way of thinking, he has unusual teaching methods but they always work very well because he does what he believes to be right. He has helped many to discover their own abilities.

On occasions Arthur has asked me to attend a class or have a reading in order to assess the quality of his students' work. On one occasion he asked Peter and me to attend a tarot class run by one of his ex-pupils and to have readings from her students. She proved to be a very fine exponent and an adept teacher of what has become known as the 'Molinary Method'. The pupils, all ladies, formed a happy and united class indeed. We each had extremely accurate readings from groups of three. A tarot reading is often helped and 'fleshed out' by using one's psychic ability as an adjunct, although it can be done without it. It is an ancient form of divination performed by reading the pictures and signs on cards and their position in relation to each other. It does not entail contacting the other world but is more concerned with telling the future and giving advice. Nonetheless, when used in conjunction with the psychic, it can be of great value.

Arthur also asked Peter and me to have readings with one of his pupils whose mediumistic ability was being tried out by the College. I found Carol Pearce to be a very pleasant, friendly lady who was obviously anxious to do her best. She started off a little tentatively but soon gathered steam. She had no idea who I was, as she was given no information except that two men would be having readings with her. She got a good contact with my mother and one or two others, but I was especially hoping to hear from certain other people. It is generally considered that when seeing a medium one should not ask questions or demand anything. From my personal experience I know differently. It is possible to ask for contact with a particular person and there is no reason why a medium can't try to do so. If the person we hope to hear from isn't there or the questions we ask cannot be answered then we must accept it. To me anything is worth a try, and for me it has worked well.

Carol agreed to try this idea and the first name I gave her was 'Betty'. After a short time she described a little lady with fair hair, all wavy and bubbly, who was surrounded by music. She felt Betty and I were close in some way and had worked together. She said Betty was excitable and extremely clever but had not achieved what she had hoped for in this world. This was a good description of someone I knew who had been a superb pianist and accompanist. She also worked in the theatre, just as Carol said. Betty and I were great friends and we wrote songs and even a musical show together. She wrote the music and I wrote the book and lyrics. She certainly never achieved the acclaim her gift warranted or had the break she truly deserved. Carol also mentioned a German link. Betty's father was originally from Germany and had also been involved in music just like his daughter. They were very close and loved each other dearly.

Next I asked if she could contact 'David' and Carol immediately described a tall young man with beautifully wavy blond hair. He was standing in front of a mirror preening himself. She told me he was very clever but sad and lonely. This was a wonderful description of David who was always fussing in front of a mirror, especially paying attention to his golden hair, which many people envied. He was indeed extremely intelligent but very sad because he never found who and what he hoped for. I helped him all I could and we had a great friendship.

The most impressive piece of evidence came, however, when Carol got hold of one of her ears and started to pull at it. She said that David was making her do it as if she was trying to pull her ear off, and that I would understand what he meant. David died of cancer of the ear at the age of forty-four. He had always had a problem with one ear which was originally diagnosed as the after-effects of a mastoid. It turned out to be cancer and as it advanced his ear became worse and, as a result of the treatment, eventually became detached. Shortly before he died we went to the cinema to see a film and the whole time we were there I was conscious of his missing ear. There were more things about other people that Carol told me but I give these two stories to illustrate the excellent evidence given through a medium trained by Arthur.

Another of Arthur's gifts is called Mexican candle reading, which is really only another way of providing something for the psychic to focus on. The psychic lights a candle, gives the recipient a sheet of paper and asks him or her to move it about gently whilst holding it over the flame. The carbon it creates makes patterns on the paper; one stops when one feels there are sufficient markings on the paper. Usually the psychic will tell you to ask a question mentally and tell him the general area of the query, for example health, work, finances, and so on. During one Mexican candle reading with

Arthur, I asked him about health and was astounded at what he was able to tell me. It was incredibly accurate and helpful. Afterwards he showed me the carbon pattern on the paper and how it clearly pinpointed the trouble about which he could have had no previous knowledge.

When Mrs Sonya Jones went to see Arthur, her mother communicated first, followed by a four or five-year-old girl. From Sonya's reaction, he detected she was more interested in the girl than her mother. Arthur said, 'I don't know what killed her but I feel as if I'm being catapulted into the air.' Sonya replied, 'She was hit by a car. She never recovered consciousness and died in a coma.' Arthur then gave a description of the girl's character and felt she was a slim blonde little girl whose main concern was about her sister, Veronika. She kept on talking about her.

Sonya was puzzled. The girl in the accident was her granddaughter and her daughter's only child. The little girl's name was Veronika. Arthur, however, persisted: 'Your granddaughter is interested in her sister Veronika.'

A year later Sonya saw Arthur again when she reminded him about her previous reading. Sonya told him that her daughter had been so grief-stricken in losing her daughter Veronika that she went to an adoption agency in Russia (she is herself Russian). She and her husband said they would like a one or two-year-old but the agency said they hadn't any girls of that age. They did, however, have a little girl, a few weeks old, who was abandoned by her mother. When they brought the child for her daughter and son-in-law to see they discovered her name was Veronika. They adopted her but changed her name to Ilona. So Veronika in the other world was quite accurate when she spoke of her 'sister' Veronika, despite her name being changed.

On one occasion a lady called Beta Razen walked into

Arthur's room for a reading. She reminded him of the Hollywood silent film star Clara Bow and was very attractive. Arthur immediately sensed she was full of sadness. When he asked, as he always does, 'Have I seen you before?' her reply was, 'I have seen the good, the bad and the ugly.' He retorted, 'Good, now you can see me!'

After studying her aura he said, 'You have a husband in the other world, he's tanned.' To which she replied, 'He's Indian.' Arthur then got a picture of him in profile and on a wall behind him were swords and other weapons. Beta commented: 'That's why and how he lost his life, in a sword fight.' When Arthur told her he felt her husband to be a caring man she replied, 'He must have changed.' Then Arthur told her: 'He is placing two jam tarts on the table in front of you.' She said, 'Every Monday he brought two home for our daughters but he was not a very generous person.' Arthur then said, 'Do you remember there was a diet drink called One Cal?' To which she said his name was Cal and then asked if he was happy now? Arthur felt he was a very serious man and not a very romantic soul, someone who wouldn't put his feelings into spoken words but wrote them down, which she acknowledged was true.

Arthur told Beta he had contact with her mother and grandmother, but before he could pass on their communications, Beta interrupted: 'They can both go to hell.' Undeterred, Arthur went on, 'You have a father in the other world,' to which she replied, 'When you get to my age, doesn't everybody?' He continued by saying her father appeared not to be a very loving man. He must have liked walking in the countryside, he thought, because he is taking me into a wood. He told her he could hear a gunshot. Did he, Arthur wondered, help himself to die? She replied, 'Yes, he shot himself in the wood, but I am proud of him for what he did because he was as mad as a hatter!'

Arthur felt her mother and father were very different

93

personalities and Beta replied bluntly, 'My mother was a slut.' Arthur described her father placing a piece of jewellery in her hand and told her it was round and long, just like a bullet. She said her father never gave her any jewellery but then pulled out a chain she was wearing and at the end of it was the bullet which had been retrieved from her father's brain. Arthur then said, 'He seems to be interested in your youngest daughter,' to which she riposted, 'He would be; she is mad as a hatter, just like him!'

At this point Arthur decided he would give her just one more thing before terminating the reading. 'Does the name Katrina mean anything to you?' At this point she went very quiet and became quite human. She said, 'Tell me more.' Arthur described a sensation which suggested Katrina was sedated and had cancer all over her body. Beta again asked him to tell her more and Arthur described a feeling of great love and friendship between the two women. In his mind he felt they were lovers but did not say it. He asked her a question: 'Did you and Katrina ever go to the Louvre in Paris?' By then the tears were rolling down her cheeks and she was wiping them off. She explained, 'That was our last trip abroad together.' Arthur relayed Katrina's message: 'My love for you is like the smile of the Mona Lisa.' Beta replied, 'She always bloody well said that to me!' At which point she stood up and left the room without a thank-you or goodbye.

Sometimes it takes a long time for the 'penny to drop'. Often messages are given where the recipients say they recognise the description of the communicator but not the relationship described by the medium. This proved to be true in the case of Michael Barley, who has consulted Arthur over a number of years. The first time they met Arthur described his mother, Betty, who was with her friend Olive Gilbert, the famous actress and musical star. Michael recognised the description but said it was that of his Aunt Betty, who

94

did indeed have a friend called Olive Gilbert, both of whom had passed on.

Michael works with a man called Phillip and they have a business which entails running and looking after property. With advice given to him from Aunt Betty and Olive they prospered and really built up their business. Michael has a young partner and Arthur always told him that although he was worried about his own health he was more concerned about his partner's health. Michael could not understand as his partner was a footballer and a very active man. But Arthur repeated he was also worried about his partner's health. Some time later his partner had a heart attack and subsequently Michael had to have a triple heart bypass, no doubt contributed to by the stress of his partner's illness.

The problems with his heart, which seemed to be genetic, led Michael to research his family history, the result of which was that he discovered his mother was in fact the lady he knew as Aunt Betty. Evidently Michael was illegitimate and after he was born his mother sent him to her sister Ann to be brought up. So finally the truth was out and Michael felt satisfied and relieved. He had received messages from his mother and, although he knew her as an aunt, when she communicated from the other world she used her correct title. His father, though, never communicated.

Arthur gave Michael more evidence and told him he would eventually pass on in Cyprus, before his partner, but both would be able to continue their work and activities for a long time yet. It seems some things remain a mystery and others eventually come to light. To those on the receiving end of such help, as Michael was, it is undeniably encouraging and helpful to feel 'one's house is more in order'.

# 11

## Gibraltar's Tercentenary and Cheryl Barrymore

As we have seen, Arthur Molinary is hailed as 'Gibraltar's own medium' and is highly respected in his home town. When he visits Gibraltar, which is as often as he can, he sees his many friends and relatives who still live there and also takes the time to give readings to the local inhabitants.

One of his readings was with the noted painter and sculptress, Sharon Keenan. He told her among other things that she would be well advised to take the commission that was being offered to her at that time, as it would prove to be an important project. This turned out to be a request for her to create the statue of Admiral Sir George Rooke to be completed in time for Gibraltar's tercentenary celebrations in 2004. Arthur received an invitation to the unveiling and felt privileged to attend this historic occasion. He had previously predicted to the columnist known as 'Dateliner' in the *Gibraltar Chronicle* that, during the unveiling ceremony, Rooke would deliver a sign to show he was pleased. At a crucial moment in the unveiling ceremony a white feather floated up from the ground and circled round the feet of the statue. Could it have come from a passing seagull or was it a sign from the admiral himself? A white feather is the traditional means of communication between a medium and a spirit. The feather could be seen on the Gibraltar Broadcasting

Corporation video and was seen by other spiritualists in the audience.

Dateliner thought it was 'very spooky', and subsequently persuaded Arthur to go on a search for ghosts and spirits around the town. Though Arthur is not especially known as a ghost-hunter, he accepted the challenge and their efforts turned up many interesting things. Most, of course, could not actually be proved, although, as many of Gibraltar's inhabitants pointed out, they often fitted in well with the known history of the place.

One such 'happening' occurred in a derelict old house in the town. An old lady had lived there, who since her youth had been waiting for her lover to return from active service in some war. Even in old age she liked to sit on the balcony where she would be able to see him walking down the street should he return. Arthur thought he had either been killed or had married someone else. Eventually the old woman died from emphysema, but to this very day she is said to be patiently waiting for his return and does her best to deter people from living in the house. All this Arthur was able to sense.

From my own experience of ghost-hunting it is difficult to prove beyond all doubt there really are ghosts, or earthbound spirits as they are often called. A medium often senses a 'reconstruction' or 're-enactment' of past events but not necessarily ghosts, so much is questionable. Whatever the truth, Arthur was showing his usual willingness to experiment and take up a challenge.


Some people are sceptical and inclined to think that mediums obtain information before the client arrives. It is as if, maybe, they suspect the College hires detectives to gather details of clients' private lives. On one occasion a lady who was seeking evidence of her husband's survival booked a reading without knowing whom she was going to see. She was very suspicious. During the reading her husband spoke of 'watching ducks fighting'. Although everything else in her reading made sense she felt this statement did not. She told him she did not live anywhere near a park pond or river. Within minutes of saying this, three ducks landed on the window sill of Arthur's room, fighting and creating an awful noise. Arthur calmly walked to the window, turned to the lady and said, 'There you are! Ducks fighting.' She gave him a faint smile and commented: 'How long did it take you to train the ducks to do that?' Taken aback he could not resist answering, with barely concealed sarcasm, 'Three months, madam.' He allowed her to leave the room believing he actually had trained the ducks! She also, however, departed with evidence of survival.

Arthur recalls an amusing incident where a lady who had had a lot of coverage on television and in the tabloid newspapers made a booking to see him. She was Cheryl Barrymore, who subsequently became Arthur's agent. The receptionists were very excited and sent her up to Arthur's room at the appointed time. He sat waiting and when she didn't appear telephoned reception, who assured him she had arrived. He waited a while longer but then went home, assuming she had changed her mind for some reason. That same afternoon he had seen another client who was a friend of Cheryl's, and when the two ladies got home they exchanged their experiences. Something did not add up. Cheryl's friend told her Arthur was tall, dark and handsome. The man Cheryl saw was short and fair. The mystery was eventually solved: Cheryl had walked up the stairs, seen a man sitting in a room with an open door and assumed it must be Arthur. She did subsequently return to have her reading with Arthur, this time being careful to enter the correct room.

It is strange how one can receive evidence, but as all mediums are different in the way they work, no story would surprise me. This can be illustrated by the time when Arthur was working at one of the College open days. His job was to inform the public about what the College did and its activities. As he went to the refreshment table for a cup of tea, a member of the public approached him and started talking. The man did not want information about Arthur and his colleagues or the services provided, but to talk about his problems and frustrations.

Listening can be an important form of therapy so Arthur stood there, prepared to do just that. In his tale of woe the man told him about his father's death and as he did so Arthur mentally felt he was flying high, as though he was in a hot-air balloon drifting across the English Channel on his way to Boulogne in France. At this point the man told him his father had fallen whilst mountain climbing in France.

Arthur continued listening to the man's story, thinking at the same time, he would buy a packet of Special K cereal on his way home. At that point the man was telling him his wife Kay had died of cancer and that she wasn't just a wife but a 'special' friend. Arthur's thoughts then turned to the days when he worked at the White City Greyhound Stadium, where the head waiter was a Mr Wallace. The man told him about his whippet, Wally, who was pining for his mistress. By listening to people and the inner self, the inner voice reaches out in a language one can understand.

All this illustrates quite clearly how psychic impressions can and do impress themselves on one's mind even if, perhaps, we do not want them. It also serves to illustrate how the people on the other side appear to use our memory bank as their 'dictionary', from which they choose the appropriate images and impressions, when communicating.

At the suggestion of a friend who had previously visited the

College, Barbara Fisher, OBE, had a reading with Arthur. Before meeting him she expected him to be wearing jeans and have a ponytail. Instead she found a smiling, well-groomed gentleman dressed in smart-casual style, with a poised and confident manner. Once he had explained the procedure for a reading, he described her aura, explaining that the emanating colours indicated some good and some not so good trends. There was time, however, to improve matters, he told her. He called her a mature lady, which she thought was a kind way to describe a 75-year-old lady.

Suddenly Arthur said her mother had come to greet her, and also a husband who was there with her mother. The husband said how sorry he was not to be able to say goodbye but wanted her to know he was always around and ready to help. Barbara found it difficult to express her feelings at that moment. Having lived with this sadness and regret for thirty-five years, to receive such words of comfort and reassurance totally transformed her memories and she suddenly experienced a wonderful feeling of peace and happiness.

Arthur then told her that she had a husband with her in this world, too. Her mother said he was an artist and told her to tell him that his next exhibition would be a success. He should paint more seascapes, she added. Barbara's mother was herself an artist and took great pleasure in following her daughter's present husband's work. Six months later the exhibition was opened. Some 250 people attended the private viewing and 71 of Clifford Fisher's paintings were sold. The success gave this fine artist the confidence and encouragement he needed to continue with his work.

Arthur's final comment to Barbara was she should be doing some writing. She protested because she found it difficult, to which he replied, in humorous vein, 'Tough!' She admits his statements and advice are always true, and usually follows them through.

Barbara's husband, Clifford, is also interested in the psychic and as a result of meeting Arthur, he invited him to sit for a portrait, which Arthur was delighted to do. This modest artist has had his paintings purchased by numerous celebrities and public figures, including the late Queen Elizabeth the Queen Mother, who had several of his pictures in her collection. The portrait of Arthur has been universally praised and now hangs in the College of Psychic Studies following its unveiling by the President, Suzanna McInerney, at a reception to celebrate Arthur's twenty years of service at the College, on 28th April 2005. It hangs next to a picture of the scientist and psychical researcher Sir Oliver Lodge, a rare honour indeed as Arthur is the only living medium to have his portrait hung in the College.

The reception was tinged with sadness because of the recent death of Cheryl Barrymore who was Arthur's friend and agent. She had done a great deal to help Arthur and had tried to launch him in his own television series. Carlton Television were very enthusiastic about the series and offered Arthur eighty daily shows, which would replace the *Richard and Judy Show*. The idea was to show Arthur giving evidence to various people of note. Unfortunately the Independent Television Commission would not give their approval, claiming it would upset the mainstream churches. Carlton took the ITC to court where Geri Halliwell and Davina McCall gave evidence in support of Arthur's programme, but the appeal was overruled. It seems the idea of mediums talking to the dead was not suitable for prime-time television, which is surprising as there are many 'psychic' programmes on satellite stations which, I feel, would upset the mainstream churches more. Perhaps eventually the idea may be taken up again, but meanwhile Arthur and many like him will continue to get the message through in whatever way they can.

# 12

## The Mind of the Medium

From my long experience in the psychic field I find that getting into the mind of a medium is one thing, but to understand how each medium works is another. It seems that most of them have different ideas and work in various ways. This is understandable since as individuals we must express ourselves in whatever way is best for our own unique approach to life, and the afterlife, in general.

I personally do not believe the gift of mediumship, or any other form of psychic expression, is something one can be taught; it is a part of one's being with which one is born, although one usually needs help in bringing it out and using it. I have always been told I am a *natural* medium, born with the gift, although when I was younger this was hard to believe as nothing remotely psychical happened until I was twenty-five. Then suddenly I became interested in the subject and was persuaded to join a 'developing class', where, the first time I attended, it was as though a switch had been pulled and I began to see and hear spirits of those who had passed to another world. It took about six months to become organised and proficient to the stage of being able to demonstrate my gift or ability, and I needed advice and help in order to achieve that.

If I am honest, I will admit to having initially copied the styles of established mediums whom I witnessed at work, but I soon realised that, although I found this worked to some extent, something within me began to feel different and I could only do it in my own way from then on. Initially I did see actual spirit forms and hear voices but it soon evolved into what is generally called mental mediumship, where one receives impressions and knows what to say and do instinctively. If I'm ever asked how it works with me, the only way I can describe it is: 'I open my mouth and speak and usually whatever I say is recognised by the recipient of the message.'

Many mediums seem to find it necessary to meditate before they work, although it really depends on personal attitude and I work better when I do not have time to think about it. In fact, some of my best demonstrations have taken place when I was running late and worried about reaching the church or hall on time. It is better for me to occupy my mind with other matters and not think about giving messages until it is necessary. It is the same with lectures on the psychic. I have often prepared notes but once I stand up and start speaking something different comes out and the notes are never used. This may sound clever but this just happens to be true of my own particular psychic gift. Having an adventurous nature I have been able to do a lot of experimenting with my gift in an effort to understand it. I like a challenge that takes me further forward; one should refuse to be beaten when it comes to a greater understanding of the subject.

There are those who are easily put down. Arthur Molinary is not one of them and one of the aims of this book has been to get into his very individual mind and try to discover exactly how his mediumship works. The psychic is a very mysterious subject and it may not be possible to get complete answers, but if we weigh the character of Arthur with what he does, it shows some very interesting aspects.

When giving a reading he says he first tunes into the 'aura' of the recipient: he sees a lot of colours which he interprets in the light of what they say about the person. Not

104

every psychic can do this but there is no doubt we all do have an aura, which might generally be described as our own personal magnetic field. I cannot see auras but since they radiate our personal feelings and power it would be true to say I can feel them and so get what is needed from them.

After tuning into the aura Arthur visualises he is in another room, each client's room being different. The room then becomes a part of their life where individual spirit communicators enter. Whether he is doing a reading inside or outside or even somewhere unusual, his mind will still be in a room. Usually the communicators come quickly and he hears them talking inside his head and not via his ears. He says he can stop them but usually lets them go on as long as is necessary. Sometimes he hears or feels things which indicate something going on *outside* the room. For example, on one occasion he told a lady that 'outside' he could hear someone singing opera. It transpired she had just started training for opera. His rooms appear sparsely furnished, perhaps with just a table and two chairs; if his communicator should put a hat, for example, on the table it is usually something symbolic which he can then interpret.

Arthur feels it is his mind he is listening to. He often refers to this by saying he is listening to 'Arturo' talking, who may or may not be his 'guide'. Arturo still speaks to him in English, unless Arthur is in Gibraltar or Spain when, after being there two or three days, he then hears him in Spanish. When he returns to England it takes the same time to revert to English. This would suggest Arthur's communications are received in pure thought form, which are then translated by his mind according to which language he is using most frequently at the time.

Arthur can shut communicators out but not 'Arturo'. He doesn't remember the readings he gives, afterwards putting it down to coming back to 'Arthur' (himself) and not the voice, 'Arturo'. He never meditates before a reading as he feels the psychic needs stimulation and there has to be something going on all the time. In an effort to 'switch off' Arthur tends to listen to the radio or watch television, so that he is listening to others and not himself. If he has a couple of drinks or a sleeping pill, it helps to block everything out, although sometimes the noises in his head seem to echo. Sometimes he hears the telephone or a doorbell ringing, which wakes him up only for him to find it is not really happening. No doubt a lot of psychics experience this sort of thing as the mind becomes ultra sensitive through the work.

Arthur has a great need to shut off after work because, despite what anyone may say, mediumistic work is mentally demanding and consequently exhausting. Many so-called experts will say the work takes something out but mediums' batteries are immediately recharged. I have never found it so but, like Arthur, find it is better to, in effect, 'change the subject' and relax. Once again the individual personality comes into this as I find it easy to shut off and have other interests to pursue. Arthur has told me that when going to sleep, if he hears the twittering of birds or is conscious of the presence of a cat or any other non-human, he becomes aware of their 'language' and they bring messages. On one occasion a bird said, 'I've got no water', whereupon he got up to discover there was no water for his pet bird. Another time the cat said, 'I'm afraid to go into the dining room'. It transpired his brother had hung a fur coat in a place where the cat would have to walk by, so the cat was afraid he would end up as a fur coat.

From my own long experience as a medium I am convinced everything comes through the mind and consequently it is important to have control of it and the intelligence to cast out that which is not right or good. The power of the mind is great, a force to be reckoned with, and when communicating with the other world it is a 'mind to mind' affair and we are responsible for not accepting what we know to be wrong. Too many mediums live in a world of fantasy and make-believe. We none of us know what this other world is like for sure, and Arthur, like myself, is intent on giving evidence of survival and help to those in need of it. There is no doubt in my mind there is a greater force outside of this world and that there is some kind of future existence, but there is no guarantee. Although Arthur provides wonderful evidence of some kind of afterlife he will only say he gives what he gets and follows his feelings, leaving it to the recipients of his readings to decide whether or not they accept his messages.

Over the years I have studied the way other people work, both in public demonstrations and private readings. Although one would initially feel they all work in the same way and on the same level, if one cares to analyse and compare, there are differences with each one. If they are asked about what they believe and how they work, some seem very confident and sure of themselves, with a tendency towards a 'I'm telling you the truth' kind of attitude. However, I doubt if anyone, myself included, has been given all the right answers. The 'spirit world', which is what it is usually called, is on another plane of existence. It is rather like landing on the moon and other planets; at one time we knew little about them but are gradually finding out more, even the possibility of there being life on them. So it is with the psychic: we can be sure that many people possess the ability to communicate with this 'other world' wherever it may be, but until we land there we will never know what it is like or where it is. Many believe death is the end and means oblivion. I personally doubt if that is so.

Over the ages countless philosophers and others have found many things to contribute to our knowledge of life itself but as yet no one has found a complete answer. Hopefully one day they will. Meanwhile those like Arthur who have a strong faith and belief in an afterlife will carry on doing what they feel compelled to do and hopefully uncover more clues which bring us nearer to the truth of 'being'.